...ERS I ✦ c.1300 – c.1600

...HERLANDISH	GERMAN	SPANISH	ENGLISH
		Influence of Siena FERRER BASSA	
...thic Art & ...rchitecture	Local Schools, Prague, Nuremberg, Hanseatic Cities, Cologne		Gothic Art & Architecture MS. Illumination
... Illumination			
...N & HUBERT ...AN EYCK			
...AMPIN ...N DER WEYDEN	STEPHAN LOCHNER		
	KONRAD WITZ	Flemish Influence	
...T ST. JANS ...RUS CHRISTUS ...RCK BOUTS ...N DER GOES ...EMLINC ...ROME BOSCH ...RARD DAVID ...PATENIER ...OSSAERT ...ASSYS	PLEYDENWURFF	HUGUET DALMAU	
	SCHONGAUER M. PACHER	BERMEJO	
	GRÜNEWALD DÜRER CRANACH ALTDORFER		
	HOLBEIN		
...TER BREUGHEL			HOLBEIN
...THONIS MOR		COELLO	
		EL GRECO	Elizabethan Portraits HILLIARD OLIVER
	ELSHEIMER		

THE OBSERVER'S BOOK OF PAINTING AND GRAPHIC ART

The Observer's Books

© FREDERICK WARNE & CO. LTD.

1958

PRINTED IN GREAT BRITAIN

THE OBSERVER'S BOOK OF

PAINTING

AND GRAPHIC ART

by

WILLIAM GAUNT

*With 16 plates in full colour
and 57 monochrome reproductions
from the original paintings*

FREDERICK WARNE & CO. LTD.

LONDON AND NEW YORK

ACKNOWLEDGEMENTS

Plates 5, 8, 12, 14, 17, 18 (*upper*), 19, 21, 24, 28, 32, 36, 40, 42, 46, 47, 49, 50, 51 and 59 (*lower*) are reproduced by courtesy of the Trustees, the National Gallery, London.

Plates 2, 7 (*upper*), 31 and 63 by courtesy of the Trustees of the Tate Gallery.

Plates 1, 13, 33 and 53 by permission of the Trustees of the Wallace Collection.

Plates 37, 41 and 45 by permission of the London County Council, Trustee of the Iveagh Bequest.

Plates 6 and 11 by courtesy of the Trustees of the British Museum.

The publishers are also indebted to the following for permission to reproduce works in their possession:

G. W. Andrews, Esq. (Plate 35); A.P.D.A.G.P., Paris (Plate 64); Sir Kenneth Clark (Plate 7, *lower*); Mrs. Julian Eisenstein (Plate 61); Earl Fitzwilliam (Plate 56); Galerie Rosengart, Lucerne (Plate 57); H. H. Levy, Esq. (Plate 23); Marlborough Fine Art Ltd. (Plate 62, *upper*); The Rochdale Art Gallery (Plate 43); The Victoria and Albert Museum (Plate 4); The Whitworth Art Gallery, Manchester (Plate 22); The Wildenstein Gallery, London (Plate 18).

While every effort has been made to trace the present owners of works reproduced, the publishers wish to apologize in advance for any inadvertent failure to make suitable acknowledgement.

PREFACE

MORE and more people today are visiting the picture galleries. Splendid exhibitions in recent years have opened the eyes of many to the endless pleasure and interest that the visual arts can afford. This little book has been designed for them as a handy reference and pocket companion.

Like music, painting and drawing can be enjoyed and appreciated without a great deal of technical knowledge. Yet to have an idea of how and why these arts have developed and flourished, what the greatest works of art have been and why they are considered so, how the artist approaches his work and with what aims, can only increase the observer's enjoyment. The attempt is made in this book to deal simply with these questions. Pointers and suggestions are offered as to how to look at pictures, and sufficient description is given of the various media used by painters and draughtsmen to assist in an understanding of the special beauties of each.

Painting, like architecture, with its roots deep in the past, is bound up with history. A brief outline is therefore given which may help the observer to distinguish the various schools and periods of painting that form so magnificent a pageant in any of the great public collections. The main themes of the painter—figure, landscape, still life, etc.—are considered separately, and masterpieces are listed and discussed under each heading.

In addition, there is a glossary of technical or special terms met with in the art world, with definitions concisely given. A biographical section on painters and draughtsmen, giving short notes on their lives and works, will be found at the end of the book and in this a selection of both old and modern masters is included.

The plates have been selected with care to illustrate as many artists, schools and styles as space will allow. Thanks are due to the public and private galleries and private owners who have granted facilities for reproduction or provided photographs of works in their possession.

W. G.

CONTENTS

LIST OF ILLUSTRATIONS

8

9

PART ONE

The Appreciation of Pictures

PAINTING, the representation of objects with some kind of pigment on a flat surface, is one of the great arts of man. It is (to use the old term of respect) one of the "Fine Arts"—this term, in its widest sense, placing together architecture, sculpture, painting, poetry and music. It implies that these are arts which are not only of practical use but appeal to the mind and the emotions in a way that is, as a famous connoisseur has put it, "life-enhancing." A great painting enriches our experience of life, just as a great poem does or a great musical composition.

Drawing, which basically means "to define a shape to the eye by putting a line round it" is inseparable from painting. The French painter Ingres described it in a striking phrase as "the probity of art": that is, as the firm and decided principle without which a work of pictorial art becomes vague and uncertain. There are of course various kinds of drawing which serve a practical purpose; but we are not here concerned with the work of the mathematical or engineering draughtsman. Nor are we concerned with graphic illustration of an informative nature but with drawing as an aspect of the artist's interest in form, with or without colour, and in its close and indeed essential connexion with the art of painting.

Historically there have been various reasons for the making of pictures, apart from the artist's desire to create a work of visual beauty. The wonderful paintings and drawings of the cave-men of the Old Stone Age were called for—there seems little doubt—as a form of magic. By depicting their quarry with an arrow in some vital spot, this hunting folk imagined they gained power over it and ensured its falling an easy victim. Some of the greatest paintings have been produced in the service of religion. At an early date the Christian Church encouraged this form of pictorial art, partly because it was understood by a multitude that could neither read nor write, and also because it could be internationally understood. "Inscribe the name of God and set up His image opposite and you will see which will be more revered," said Leonardo da Vinci in a famous comparison of the arts.

Painting has also been used as propaganda for the state and to serve as a reminder of its power and magnificence. A great number of imposing works of this order were produced during the 17th century, while the tradition of royal portraiture has continued in Europe at least from medieval times to the present day. From this point of view pictorial art is a very valuable historical record. Holbein, for instance, preserves for us the features of Tudor royalty and members of the court and gives us besides much precise information as to their costume and jewellery.

There are many more purposes which have called pictures into being. The taste of particular classes of patrons has required a variety of subjects, for example, the representations of classical fables which delighted the princes of the Renaissance in Italy or the paintings of flowers and fruits which appealed to the Dutch burghers and horticulturists of 17th century Holland. Pictures have been painted with an improving or ethical purpose and this was ostensibly the motive of Hogarth's series of subject pictures, though as works of art they are valued on other grounds. Since the early 19th century more and more pictures have been painted, not for a patron, but because of some need felt by the artist to express his own thoughts and feelings, and this communication of thought and feeling of an individual kind is one of painting's most important functions.

Thus there are many reasons why the study of painting is worth while. It is one of the most valuable companions to history, illuminating life and ideas in all parts of the world and at all periods. Yet great art is not great because it imparts information. The masterpieces of painting, like the masterpieces of music and poetry, transform experience; they are an inexhaustible source of beauty which is different from what we call the "beauty of nature" and derives from the originality of the artist's outlook, his gift of perception and quality of mind, his capacity for combining form and colour into a harmonious unity. Great painters in their own way teach us to see, not simply the observable facts, but with something of their own imagination. Thus James McNeill Whistler, in his famous *Nocturnes* of the Thames, communicates his own appreciation of the river and twilight in a way that has enabled many people to look at such a scene through his eyes. No one indeed, to judge by the first unfavourable reception of his *Old Battersea Bridge* (Pl. 2), had previously had an inkling of the beauty he found. Whistler's saying, on one occasion: "Nature is creeping up to Art", wittily expressed the fact that art trains the senses and in a way decides how nature appears to our vision.

In studying painting, then, it is as well to dismiss first of all the idea that there is one standard of correctness or accuracy to which all artists must be expected to conform. We must not demand topographical accuracy from the landscape painter. Turner, for example, freely rearranges the elements in a view to suit his composition and is quite capable of converting a mound of moderate size into a mountain if he thinks it will help the general effect. The figure painter, in the same way, is not prohibited from exaggeration and distortion if the effect he has in mind requires it. That great genius of the Italian Renaissance, Michelangelo, whose study and knowledge of anatomical structure were very thorough, often takes surprising liberties and gives to his figures disproportionately large and muscular limbs: though this as part of the total effect is not an awkwardness or imperfection, but contributes to its majesty and grandeur. Again, in paintings by the 16th century Spanish master El Greco, there is an obvious elongation of the figures which at one time was put down to some defect in the painter's eyesight. Yet this could not be so, because, when he wished, El Greco proved himself perfectly capable of depicting a figure of normal proportions. It is clear, as present-day criticism recognizes, that his "flame-like" forms were in harmony with the intensely spiritual feeling of his work. People sometimes point out faults of perspective in paintings or drawings, but these are not necessarily faults. Perspective is more properly a matter of science than of art. As such it was eagerly taken up by the scientifically minded painters of the Italian Renaissance, for example by the Florentine painter Paolo Uccello; though his wonderful *Rout of San Romano* in the National Gallery in London has a chivalrous, fairy-tale character which owes very little to this particular science. There are works by medieval and oriental artists which disregard perspective to the positive advantage of their design.

Let us imagine that six painters make a picture of the same bowl of fruit. It is safe to say that each of these pictures will be different from the others. It can also be stated that this does not mean that one of the paintings is "right" and all the rest are wrong, or alternatively that all of them are wrong; but that each of them has a different way of looking at things, a different "artist-personality" (cf. Pl. 62). Even so simple a form as an apple, when painted by the French artist Cézanne (Pl. 3), is at once distinguishable from an apple painted by his fellow-countryman Courbet. The element of personality

15

gives its endless diversity to art and this diversity is an essential part of its fascination.

In what, then, does the special skill of the artist consist? It is not the skill of the copyist, but that knowledge and command of his materials which enables the artist to express what he wishes. There are obviously exacting disciplines involved. The early works of great artists show their anxiety to acquire perfect manual skill and the faculty of re-producing in a convincing manner what is before their eyes. According to tradition, Giotto, one of the greatest Italian artists, advanced, as evidence of his skill, a perfect circle, drawn freehand, thus demonstrating his entire certainty of hand. The early interior scenes painted by the great Spaniard Velazquez are marvels of precise detail. The early water-colours of Turner, hard and factual, are in surprising contrast with the daring freedom of his later years. In each, however, the first stage is the least personal: what we value in them most is not a mechanical dexterity or their youthful "diploma pieces" but the mature expression of their individuality.

In so far as painting is to be looked on as a craft, it has certain rules which represent the traditional wisdom of the craftsman. There are, for instance, certain approved ways of using the artist's media (which will be considered in some detail in the next section). There are rules of composition tending to give unity and coherence to the work as a whole. A master would often base an elaborate subject picture on some elementary or geometrical shape.

Thus famous pictures, containing the various forms of human beings, trees, buildings, etc., may have an entirely abstract foundation and derive their unity from it. An abstract device of this kind is the triangular or pyramidal composition which gives the effect of stability and repose. A division of the picture space diagonally tends to give breadth and vigour. William Hogarth the "father of English painting", in his *Analysis of Beauty* arrived at what he called the "line of beauty," the serpentine line which could be produced by winding a piece of wire round a cone, and this gives an implied graceful movement to some of his own paintings.

The unifying factors of composition have three aspects. There is the linear, surface design; the balance of light and shade which concerns the impression or illusion of depth and three dimensions; and composition in colour. Harmony of colour is observed to result from the repetition of the same colours in various parts of a picture. There are numerous ways of ensuring an agreeable contrast and balance by the relative placing of areas of warm and cool colour.

These are aspects of what may be called the science of picture making. In themselves they do not automatically create a great picture. A minor artist may use them as knowingly as a master, yet they will not enable him to attain the master's stature. Similarly they are not the main way to appreciation. One might in a parallel fashion study Shakespeare's tricks of stagecraft, and perhaps gain some extra appreciation of him as a man versed in the theatre, and of the effective construction of a play, without, however, understanding *Hamlet* any better! Attempts have been made to analyse great pictures by means of diagrams showing their principles of construction and these are often interesting and may be well-founded; but they merely reveal the skeleton, and what concerns us is the warm flesh-and-blood, the living intelligence of art. Primarily the science of picture making is for the artist and not the spectator, though the spectator is not to be discouraged from acquiring some general idea of the pictorial science. He certainly must be prepared to enjoy form and colour without concentrating solely on subject matter or incidental items of human interest—and to that extent to share the approach of the artist himself.

A picture is, or should be, an interesting shape as a whole, to be first looked at as an *object* before we think about its *subject*. The French painter-critic Maurice Denis put this emphatically in the following way: "A picture—before being a war-horse, a nude woman or any subject whatever—is essentially a plane surface covered with colours assembled in a certain order." This is the more important because we are bound in the first place to take in the picture as a whole. Its effect is not built up over a period of time like that of a book we read or a piece of music to which we listen. We have to stand back from it so that we can see instantaneously how its colours and forms are related and interact. Subsequently, of course, we can examine more closely this portion or that in detail, and this is a process which reveals many further delights and subtleties. It is one of the advantages of present-day photography that it can isolate and enlarge for us beautiful details which would be lost in a small reproduction of an entire picture. The film too has made its contribution by photographing a series of different parts of a great picture so that its movement or rhythm can be appreciated in consecutive phases. To sum up, we look first to the completeness of the artist's conception and then to the variety it contains, the quality of the paint, brushwork and drawing and the way in which these qualities are fused with the subject matter.

We have already gone some way towards defining what it is that makes a masterpiece. It is not subject alone. An artist is not more original because he has some unusual story to tell, and any of the great collections will show how well content the masters have been with subjects that have been treated again and again by many different hands. It is the way it is done and what the artist brings to the subject that counts. A great work of art is truly a creation in that it lives with a life of its own. We cannot really separate form and content—they have grown together and become one in the creative process. Together with this vital consistency a masterpiece possesses the endless interest of life itself. The more we look at it the more it reveals and this is not necessarily because of the amount of detail and incident it contains. A still life by the French 18th-century painter Chardin, composed of a few simple objects, is inexhaustible in its fascination because it is filled with a great artist's sense of the mystery and wonder of all form.

There is no exact system by which we can immediately detect a great work, and attempts to formulate a rigid canon of judgement have never been wholly satisfactory. Thus Sir Joshua Reynolds in the *Discourses* he gave as President of the Royal Academy constructed a system based on what he termed the "Grand Style". He described this as consisting primarily in some dignified or lofty subject in which an ideal type of humanity was depicted; and secondly in the exclusion of all particular or descriptive detail which might divert attention from the general beauty of form. For example, anything in the nature of fashion in dress did not conform to the Grand Style, but destroyed its timeless and universal character. Thus Raphael clothed his figures in garments that vaguely suggest the classical world but have no specific date (Pl. 4). It followed from Reynolds' ideas that a Flemish picture of low life was necessarily inferior to the grander themes painted by the Italian Renaissance masters.

Yet while there is much of value in Reynolds' system of criticism it is impossible to apply it today without a great many reservations. The realists of the 19th century produced splendid works in which there was a deliberate refusal to idealize humanity. Landscape in which human figures might not appear at all was shown to be capable of greatness. Raphael or Michelangelo and Titian are masters to whom we give homage without question, just as in the field of literature we acknowledge the greatness of Shakespeare or Milton, or in music of Bach or Mozart. This does not mean, however, that all other painters must paint in the same style, or choose the same subjects. Even in the past there have been original artists who were long neglected because they were unlike the accepted notion of the great artist. It is, for instance, only in comparatively recent times that such masters as El Greco of Toledo and Vermeer of Delft have been recognized for their true value and accorded their proper place among the foremost representatives of European art.

Taste is not, indeed, a fixed quantity. In little more than half a century the world has seen a surprising change in the appreciation of painters like Paul Cézanne and Vincent Van Gogh who towards the end of the 19th century, when they were at the height of their production, were either ignored or angrily derided. The reason for their unpopularity was the difficulty people found in adjusting their vision to a new view of things. These painters were in advance of their time: without the particular prejudices of that time or its habitual way of looking at pictures, a later generation has been able to understand them perfectly well.

The appreciation of pictures is not a special faculty which only a few can possess. The habit of looking at good pictures is in itself a means by which taste can be formed and the scope of one's enjoyment widened and developed. The world as a whole has understood art much better since exhibitions and reproductions have made a larger variety of great works available to more people than ever before. If we had lived in the 18th century our enjoyment of art would probably have been limited to the products of Europe in a period of some two hundred years, the "old master" age of the 15th to 17th centuries. We should have known the 16th and 17th century masters Titian, Velazquez, Rembrandt and Rubens, and this certainly implies that we should have had excellent works to study. Yet how much broader appreciation has since become. It was the critical achievement of the 19th century to reveal wondrous regions of art that had previously been unknown or ignored. The early Italian painters were discovered and their beauty of design and colour was properly assessed. Next the enthusiasm of certain artists and critics made Europe aware that it was not unique in painting and drawing: that the East also had produced great works not merely exotic or unintelligible but with recognizable and delightful qualities beneath their unfamiliar first appearance. The Japanese print and Chinese landscape have added to and enriched our outlook (Pl. 11).

We have also come to realize, through more recent studies, that painting and drawing are something more than professional competence: that they have a deep significance and special interest as the natural expression of mind and personality. The extraordinary pictures made by children and by the unschooled adult "primitives" are types of art which show in a striking way this operation of natural instinct. We do not look for masterpieces among them, yet they too enlarge our view by demonstrating the part that spontaneous expression can play, as well as conscious skill and matured intelligence.

The general effect of these varied discoveries has been to show how universal and how deep-rooted an instinct is art. It is also a language that knows no frontiers and is independent of space and time. By its means we can communicate with those of another race or another period as well as learn what our contemporaries feel about the world we live in. The wider perspective opened in the last hundred years has made it possible for the art lover to enjoy the variety of technique, treatment and subject that the whole of history offers, and to feel that it contains an underlying unity.

PART TWO

The Character and Uses of the Artist's Media

EACH of the media employed by the painter and draughtsman has its own fitness for some special purpose, and intrinsic qualities of its own which affect the final result. It is useful, therefore, for the observer to have at least a general idea of their nature and the techniques associated with them.

Let us take drawing first, as the basic form of pictorial art. The purposes of drawing are several. It may be a study of nature, or an exercise, made by the artist for its own sake. Or it may be a preliminary sketch for a painted composition, or a study of detail to be used in a painting. It may sometimes be highly finished, like the wonderful portrait drawings of Holbein (Pl. 6) which were probably intended to give the sitter a fairly exact idea of how a portrait commission would turn out when finally completed in paint. Broadly speaking, however, a drawing is intended to suggest rather than to be complete (though even an outline may in a remarkable way give the impression of rounded and three-dimensional form). In a drawing we come nearest to an artist's process of thought and method of creation: which is one of the reasons why connoisseurs—and artists wealthy enough to be so—have in the past accumulated large collections of drawings by various hands and treasured them as highly as paintings. In drawing, the artist is able to be most free, spontaneous and direct. He has at his command a number of media contributing to this end, each possessing special qualities.

PEN DRAWING

The quill or reed pen was a favourite instrument of the old masters who valued the ease, vigour and precision of effect which it could give. They generally used a black ink (which has often turned brown with age) together with a warm pigment, e.g. bistre (a preparation of wood-soot) or sepia (originally from the "ink" of the cuttle-fish). The line was often reinforced by a wash of the warm monochrome, broadly mapping out light and shade. In this way an artist could swiftly set down the essentials either of a composition or of a single object of study. Modern drawings for reproduction, executed with a steel pen and intensely black ink, belong to a different category, and while they are often brilliant in their way, they cannot fairly be compared with the drawings in which the old masters were free to set down the essentials of their thought and vision.

SILVERPOINT

This was the method of drawing extensively used before the "lead pencil" was devised. A point of silver or other metal, on paper coated with a surface of zinc white, produced a grey line similar to that made by a lead pencil but of much greater delicacy. Drawings by Dürer and Leonardo (Pl. 6), for example, show how well suited its delicacy was to portraits of women and children. It is little used today partly because of its small and delicate range.

PENCIL AND CHALK

Since the 18th century the graphite pencil has been generally used both for making rapid notes of outline and to some extent for indicating light and shade—though pencil shading, if carried too far, becomes smudgy and shiny. It is useful to the artist as a subsidiary aid rather than as a main form of expression, though it may possess exquisite quality, as is shown in the superb portrait drawings by Ingres.

Hard chalk, however, is a superior medium, capable of precision but with a broader range in its suggestion of form and colour. Masterpieces in black chalk or red (sanguine) or a combination of the two have been produced by such great painters as Raphael, Holbein, Rubens, Watteau and Gainsborough. The figure studies by Watteau in black and red chalk rival his oil paintings in beauty.

CHARCOAL AND PASTEL

Charcoal is used for drawing on canvas preparatory to oil painting, but as it can easily be rubbed out it has not been extensively used for finished drawings, though it gives richness of shadow and a varied strength of line. Titian and Tintoretto used it with white chalk on coloured paper, and there is a magnificent charcoal drawing of a young man by Dürer in the British Museum.

Pastel is a soft chalk, which, like charcoal, requires a fixative to be made permanent. It may be regarded as a medium either for drawing or for painting with dry colour, for its wide range of colours is its main asset, and, not being diluted with a liquid medium, the colours possess unusual brilliance. In this respect they may excel those of oil painting as in the direct and vigorous pastels of the 19th-century French artist Degas (Pl. 7).

BRUSH DRAWING

The use of the brush as a means of outlining or determining shape brings us to the intermediate ground between drawing and painting. The art of prehistoric cave-man developed from simple outline with a certain amount of shading or modelling of form. From his studies at Altamira in Spain the Abbé Breuil, celebrated expert on prehistoric art, concluded that brushes of various sizes and kinds were used. The vase painting of the ancient Greeks is in effect a free and spirited form of drawing with a brush. The sensitive response of the brush to pressure is beautifully illustrated by the work of Oriental artists, Chinese and Japanese, who can swiftly and unerringly create a picture with a few strokes. There is the same calligraphic sense in a remarkable series of brush drawings of artist and model by Pablo Picasso.

WATER-COLOUR PAINTING

The various forms of painting are distinguished by the vehicle with which the pigment is used.

Thus water-colour consists of pigments bound with gum and diluted with water. In essence, the brush drawings of the Far East are water-colour, and an ancient example is that of Egyptian paintings on papyrus; though we usually think of water-colour as a development in Europe from the wash drawings that have been previously mentioned, and more especially as an English art. The old masters used mainly a monochrome wash, though they occasionally added to it a slight tint of positive colour. Some Dutch painters, like Ostade (1610–1685), tinted pen drawings of figure subjects, but the art was first highly developed in later 18th-century England. In its first phase it may be called water-colour drawing, being an accompaniment to a careful pen or pencil drawing. Sometimes colour was lightly applied over a work carefully finished in monochrome, but the trend in the early 19th century was towards the direct use of positive colour in water-colour painting

Water-colour became widely used through the growth of interest in topography and landscape. It provided a suitable original from which engravings in topographical books could be made. It was also the most convenient medium for the travelling artist, much of whose work was done in the open, as it lends itself to swift notation. A great asset of water-colour is the luminous quality resulting from the shine of the white paper ground through a transparent wash. It is best when swiftly applied and least retouched, being suggestive in the same way as drawing; though for the same reason it **can** never rival the completeness of oil painting. Thus water-colour painting can suggest the movement and animation of a crowd—Thomas Rowlandson (1756–1827) gives some excellent examples—but cannot adequately give solid modelling to the human form. On this account some critics have denied its greatness as an art, considering it necessarily sketchy and imperfect, and tending to a superficial prettiness.

Nevertheless such English water-colourists as J. R. Cozens, Girtin (Pl. 22), Cotman and Bonington have a high place in the history of landscape painting and Turner (1775–1851) raises water-colour to the peak of expressive capacity. The quality of a medium, we must always remember, depends on the quality of the artist who uses it. Some of Turner's most astonishing "chromatic poems" are executed in water-colour, while among artists more recent in date Cézanne (1839–1906) is as magnificent in water-colour as in oil.

Some artists have given greater solidity to the medium by the use of what is called "body colour" or "gouache", that is, water colour mixed with an opaque white. Turner achieves superb results with body colour on a toned paper. Gainsborough sometimes uses a fascinating mixture of chalk drawing, transparent wash and touches of opaque colour. An historical use of opaque water colour, to be considered apart, is in the illuminated manuscripts of the Middle Ages, and a survival of this technique is to be seen in the portrait miniature on parchment or ivory.

Water-colour is adapted to work on a small scale. Until the 15th century complete pictures of a fairly large size, intended to occupy some decorative or fixed place in relation to architecture, were carried out in tempera. The vehicle of tempera was usually yolk of egg diluted with water as required. The painting was done on a coating of gesso, a fine white plaster covering a wooden panel or canvas. As it dries quickly, it necessitates a special technique involving the use of separate strokes or a sort of line work with a brush for shading and detail. The beauty of tempera can best be appreciated in the work of the Italian masters up to and including the Italian Renaissance. The serenity, the well-defined linear character, the purity of clear colour, seen for example in Piero della Francesca's *Baptism of Christ* in the National Gallery, are the qualities to be looked for. With the introduction of oil painting, artists aimed at a greater richness of effect by the use of transparent films or glazes of oil paint over tempera. The two unfinished paintings by Michelangelo in the National Gallery are admirable illustrations of the method (Pl. 5). Some praiseworthy modern attempts to revive tempera have been made but it has been very largely superseded by oil painting which has greater resource and can be used with more freedom.

FRESCO

Fresco is the traditional method of painting directly on to the interior walls of a building.

Colours are mixed with water and applied on a layer of lime plaster while this is still fresh. The colour, thus combined with, and drying with, the plaster, becomes a permanent part of the fabric. The method is even more exacting than that of tempera, with which it has some elements in common. It necessitates quick and decided handling and does not allow of retouching. The paint dries with a mat surface and effect is gained rather by the bold definition of masses and purity of colour than by depth, light and shade and richness of colour. Elaborate preliminaries were usual and the old masters were in the habit of transferring a complete full size version or "cartoon" of the design to the wall in outline by tracing or pouncing.

The ancient world knew the method, but its main pictorial use in Europe dates from the beginning of the great period of church building in the 12th century. The Romanesque churches had much wall space that could appropriately be devoted to paintings of religious themes: but the development of Gothic architecture in western and northern Europe, with its greatly enlarged window spaces and manifold divisions of wall area, caused the decline of fresco in this region and the cultivation of the comparatively small and detailed altarpiece. Italy, on the other hand, where the Gothic style never gained much hold, continued to offer the painter suitable wall-space, and the light and warmth of the climate also provided favourable background conditions. A long succession of painters produced masterpieces in fresco, from Giotto's famous series of the Life of Christ and the Life of the Virgin at Padua (1303) to the *Last Judgement* by Michelangelo in the Vatican (1534–40).

The rise of oil painting led to the extinction of fresco. Leonardo da Vinci experimented with a mixed method involving the use of oil for his *Last Supper* but this proved woefully impermanent. Modern wall-painting is to be distinguished from fresco, being generally executed on canvas in the same way as the portable oil "easel picture" and then fitted into place in the interior scheme.

PAINTING WITHOUT BRUSHES

An account of the artist's media would not be complete without reference to methods of historical importance in which the brush is not used at all, or plays only a minor part. One such method is that of encaustic (burning in) used by the Greco-Roman artists of the Imperial age. Coloured wax was the medium, and the main part of the work was done with melted wax applied with a spatula—a process to some extent comparable with the palette-knife painting of certain modern artists. Its permanence, solidity, and the peculiarly incisive quality which artists were able to attain by its means, can be appreciated from the portraits painted on mummy cases in Egypt of the Roman period, of which there are masterly examples in the National Gallery (Pl. 8).

Mosaic has also been an equivalent of painting in conjunction with architecture. The famous Byzantine mosaics of the Emperor Justinian, the Empress Theodora and their court in the church of S. Vitale,

1. SIR JOSHUA REYNOLDS
Nelly O'Brien

2. JAMES MCNEILL WHISTLER
Nocturne—Old Battersea Bridge

3. PAUL CÉZANNE
Still Life

4. RAPHAEL: Cartoon—*Paul and Barnabas rejecting the sacrifice
offered to them at Lystra*

5. Michelangelo
The Entombment

HANS HOLBEIN: *Portrait Drawing*

LEONARDO DA VINCI: *Bust of a Warrior*
(silverpoint)

6.

VINCENT VAN GOGH: *View at Auvers*

7. EDGAR DEGAS: *Woman at the Wash Basin*

8. GRECO-ROMAN PAINTING
Portrait of a Young Woman

Photo: Mansell

Church of San Vitale, Ravenna

9. MOSAIC: *The Empress Theodora and her Court*

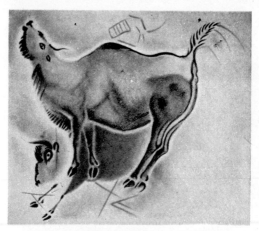

PREHISTORIC CAVE PAINTING: *Bellowing Bison, Altamira*

10. REMBRANDT: *The Sow* (etching)

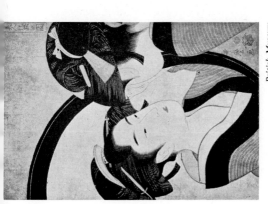

British Museum

CHINESE PAINTING of Sung
Dynasty: *Tiger*

British Museum

11. JAPANESE COLOUR PRINT
(UTAMARO): *Woman Before a Mirror*

National Gallery, London

12. PETER PAUL RUBENS: *Peace and War*

13. J. H. FRAGONARD
   The Swing

14. HANS MEMLINC
Young Man at Prayer

15. WILLIAM HOLMAN HUNT: *The Hireling Shepherd*

16. PAUL GAUGUIN: *Te Rerioa*

Ravenna (6th century A.D.), can justly be regarded as superb examples of pictorial art (Pl. 9). The combination of variously coloured pieces of stone or glass to produce this pictorial result has an interesting likeness to the method of the later Impressionist painters whose paintings are virtually a "mosaic" of patches of pure colour placed side by side and fusing together when seen at a distance.

Stained glass, it may also be noted, was the equivalent of a picture in the church of the Middle Ages, providing a majestic design and colour scheme. The amount of painting with a brush was here strictly limited, the supremely important factor being the rich glow of the translucent material and the decorative outline of the strips of leading which held it together.

These are historical reminders of the variety of techniques that artists may use for a pictorial end: we have left to the last perhaps the most important medium of all and certainly the most highly regarded in modern times, that of oil painting.

OIL PAINTING

Oil paints are pigments bound with oil and diluted as required with linseed oil or turpentine, or both in combination. This medium has a more extensive range than any that have been described. Not confined by the special limitations of tempera or fresco, it can be used with entire freedom. At the same time, if the artist desires, it can, with due precautions, be worked on again and again, and in this respect it has a clear advantage. The scope of oil painting may be described as orchestral. It can achieve a delicate and transparent effect, or the greatest strength and richness, rivalling even the glow of stained glass. It lends itself to broadly executed work on a huge scale or to minutely detailed work on an area of a few square inches. No other medium offers such varied possibilities in the use of both transparent and opaque pigments.

It would be hard to say when oil-painting was "invented", but it was first extensively practised in the Netherlands and Germanic lands during the 14th century, partly no doubt because it was more resistant than other media to a rigorous or damp climate. The Flemish master Jan van Eyck, however, showed that the medium was not merely serviceable from this point of view but could attain a wonderful brilliance. He and his Flemish contemporaries cultivated the transparent method, painting on a white gesso ground which gave a clear and luminous quality to the pigment, the picture being carefully and smoothly finished, piece by piece. The picture was dried in the sun so as to extract the surplus oil which might have yellowed and darkened with time. The perfection of surface and the inner life of colour (like that of certain precious stones) are qualities of which one is always aware in looking at a picture by Jan van Eyck, and have given rise to the belief that he possessed some magic recipe, the secret of which has been lost. It seems likely, however, that the recipe was no more than the method that has here been described, pursued with the unhurried system and thoroughness of the master-craftsman. In the 19th century the Pre-Raphaelites used a method somewhat resembling that of the early painters in oils, painting thinly on a white ground before it was entirely dry, and finishing one piece at a time, thus attaining that brilliance of colour which so surprisingly distinguishes their works from other paintings of the Victorian age.

The Flemish method of transparent painting was transported to Italy, where, as we have noted in paintings by Michelangelo, the glazes of oil colour were applied over a tempera underpainting. The works of the Venetian painter Giovanni Bellini, in the 15th century, may be compared with those of van Eyck in beauty of surface and enamel-like colour; yet painters did not feel that the full possibilities of the medium had yet been explored. In the 16th and 17th centuries there was a change of method which sought to take full advantage of both the opaque and transparent values of the oil medium. The picture was now first carefully laid in, in monochrome. The light parts of a picture, instead of being more thinly painted than the rest, were painted with opaque and thicker colour. Being slightly raised above the level of the canvas, this thicker pigment took a sparkle of light from the natural light in which it was viewed while the slight shadow it cast gave an additional life and variety to the surface. The shadows, on the other hand, were painted thinly, and the application of successive glazes of transparent colour gave a glowing depth which had not been obtainable before. Titian is the first great exemplar of this method. With him it was a long-drawn-out and elaborate process, each successive application of colour being allowed to dry thoroughly and being exposed to the sun to remove the superfluity of oil before the next was put on. Thus he was able to combine the brilliance of colour attained by earlier artists with a variety of surface, a depth and a rich modelling of form that was unprecedented in art.

Broadly speaking, here we have the "classic" method of oil painting, though it allowed for a great deal of variation (Titian's own procedure altered in his later years). Some great painters have worked mainly in transparent colour on a thickly painted monochrome ground—Rembrandt, for instance, did so, though he also forced up an effect of high lights with a heavy load of pigment as required. When we look at his pictures we feel the living quality of substance thus produced, even while we may be thinking of something so different as the psychology of his portraiture.

Other masters, for example Frans Hals and Velazquez, have used opaque and transparent colour freely and directly, dispensing with the leisurely process of building up a picture in successive stages, with a resultant gain in the vividness and personality of handling. If one studies the details of an Infanta's dress by Velazquez, one sees how the surface is animated by this directness of touch.

When painters in the 19th century came to work from nature in the open air, one can see why an increasing directness was necessary, and also a further alteration in technique. To the Impressionists, the differences of light and shade were differences of colour, and therefore they painted with a fairly uniform density of pigment, constructing a picture from patches of pure colour laid side by side. Clearly the freshness of effect at which they aimed could not be achieved either by the precise finish of the early Flemings or the elaborate calculation of the Venetians. Then again, when we look at the work of Vincent van Gogh, we can hardly fail to notice that the emphatic strokes of the brush heavily loaded with pigment take on a sort of tempestuous movement which is related to the intensity of his emotion (Pl. 7). Oil painting, in fact, is infinitely adaptable as a mode of expression. Some people regret that modern artists freely depart from the classic method of building up a picture on a monochrome basis, yet the method has always varied in one way or another, and these variations are to be appreciated as part of painting's inexhaustible store of interest.

DISEASES OF PAINTING

Perhaps the main drawback of oil painting as a medium is its susceptibility to chemical change, cracking and darkening. The observer is constantly struck by the fact that paintings of some age vary enormously in the condition in which they have come down to us. Tempera does not suffer from time to nearly the same extent as oil, nor does water-colour, suitably protected from strong sunlight. Time is not entirely to blame—one can only marvel that encaustic portraits more than fifteen hundred years old or Flemish pictures some five hundred years old remain unaffected by age. Yet even great artists have sometimes been careless in their use of their medium. Some of Sir Joshua Reynolds' works, for instance, have been ruined by his injudicious use of asphaltum, a species of bituminous varnish. Mixed with paint, it gave an extra richness, but has set up an unending chemical reaction with dire results. The colour of Leonardo's *Mona Lisa* is not as it left the artist's hand, because he used a fugitive madder in some parts of the flesh which has disappeared. Varnish, floated over a picture to preserve it, is in many cases the cause of a dark, cracked and yellowed appearance. The prevalence of this varnish has given rise to a popular impression that "old masters" were deliberately sombre in tone. When pictures in public collections have been cleaned, and the darkened varnish removed, the effect has sometimes been disconcertingly bright to eyes accustomed to the previous mellowness. The fact that they were painted in a more brilliant key than has been supposed should not, however, be a barrier to appreciation; on the contrary one may be put in mind of Hogarth's words when writing of the effects of time and varnish: "In a landscape, will the water be more transparent or the sky shine with a greater lustre when embrowned and darkened by decay?"

PART THREE

Periods, Schools and Styles

PRIMITIVE ART

IT is essential for the observer to have at least an outline background of the historical development of pictorial art, and to take first a brief glance at its prehistoric and primitive forms. All the arts have their origin in prehistoric times, but the representations of animals incised on ivory and bone or drawn and painted on the walls and ceilings of caves in the north of Spain and south of France still excite wonder by their exceptional power and "modernity" (Pl. 10). Masterpieces were produced between (to give very rough limits) 40,000 B.C. and 10,000 B.C. What we notice in the photographs or outline copies made from them is the way in which the artist has selected and emphasized the main characteristics of the animals—mammoth and bison, deer, wild boar and wild horse—depicted; the knowledge he displays of their anatomy; the solid bulk and vigorous movements he conveys with no more than a little black and red ochre.

The period during which they were produced is longer than all recorded history, but there are comparable paintings and drawings by people living a similar life at a much later date. Thus the

African bushman has left, in rock-shelters, drawings of animals as beautiful as those of our first European artists and resembling them in style, though some are as recent as the 19th century of our era. The realism of these hunting folk is not repeated in the art of the next stage of civilization, when social life takes a more definite form, when tools of stone and bronze are perfected, the crafts of pottery and weaving are pursued and, with the growth of agriculture, various rites and ceremonies propitiating the elements come into being. The typical primitive society, of which there still remain various survivals as in Polynesia, is largely concerned in the arts with its rudimentary religion. Carving and sculpture exceed painting in importance: the idol in three dimensions more impressively represents the powers assumed to affect primitive life. Painting and drawing are reduced to a series of signs and symbols. This, in a way, seems a step backwards from the art of the cave-man though it must be remembered that the latter was less well organized. The cave-man could draw a single animal superbly: he had not yet learnt to set a group in ordered relation— often one image is superimposed on another in the most heedless way. It is with the later primitive society that the idea of painting as decoration comes into being.

THE ANCIENT MEDITERRANEAN WORLD

Painting and drawing in the ancient Mediterranean world have three aspects. There is first the wall painting, with bold outline and flat colour, the technique somewhat resembling that of certain modern posters. The ancient Egyptians used it on the exteriors of their temples: a sharply defined low relief providing an outline which was filled with bright colour. The majority of surviving Egyptian paintings are those of tomb walls, including scenes from the life of the deceased. A number of conventional devices are regularly used, for example, the male figure is painted in red ochre, the female, in yellow; the head and legs are always in profile however otherwise the body is turned. A great quality, however, is the lively observation which appears in scenes of banqueting and dancing or fishing and fowling along the Nile. The wall paintings of ancient Crete discovered in the palace of Knossos afford a parallel with those of Egypt in their bright, flat colours and decided outlines, though entirely secular in character.

The painted pottery of ancient Greece offers on a small scale something of these traditional styles. The male figure is dark, the female figure light, and outline plays a dominant part. The Greek vase painters (who often signed their cups and vases) can be studied as draughtsmen with a most exquisite sense of value of line and silhouette. In the classical period, however, the art of vase painting ceased to occupy an important place, and it is now that we first come upon the record of pictures in the modern sense, though our idea of them is unfortunately not based on the authentic works of the legendary masters, Zeuxis or Apelles, but on copies of Greek painting discovered when the Roman cities Pompeii and Herculaneum were excavated. It is clear enough however, that the Greek painters had given the art a scope and character undreamed of by the Egyptians or Minoans. Their work was no longer flat, but represented light and shade. The Greeks conceived dramatic figure compositions: they interested themselves in the problem of giving individual character and expression to their figures, in features and gesture. The Greco-Roman works that adorned the villas of wealthy Romans in the 1st century A.D. provide examples of landscape (previously unknown) and of still-life studied for its own sake. They forecast the later development of painting in Italy.

BYZANTINE ART

The dissolution of the Roman Empire, the establishment of a new Rome in the former Byzantium (Constantinople), and the emergence of Christianity as the universal creed of the West gave to painting a new character, spirit and aim. The Christian religion was now the artist's theme. A formal style now known as Byzantine, suited to express its earnestness and ritual, grew up. Constantinople had many links with the East, whose influence is to be seen in the use of rich colour.

The main triumphs of Byzantine pictorial art were achieved in mosaic, on the walls or the curved surface of the inner domes of the Byzantine church. Its other forms were, firstly, the icon, the image of Christ or the Virgin, represented, of set purpose, in a fixed convention which in itself declared the unalterable nature of belief; and secondly the illumination of manuscript Gospels and liturgical works with painting and gold. The style of these is as unchanging as that of the icon.

The Byzantine capital remained intact, prosperous and fixed in its ways for 1,100 years after its foundation in the 4th century A.D., so that works, very similar in many respects, may vary considerably in date. The sphere of Byzantine art corresponds to the sphere of influence of the Byzantine Empire: the eastern shores of the Mediterranean, Greece and the Greek islands. To some extent it was carried westward, with the movements of Byzantine missionaries and craftsmen. The famous 8th-century Irish manuscript, the Book of Kells, has its links of style with the eastern Mediterranean. The Italian cities Florence, Siena and Pisa had a Byzantine tradition, the end of which is marked by the painting of Cimabue in Florence and Duccio in Siena in the 13th century. In eastern Europe what is now Yugoslavia has remarkable Byzantine wall paintings of the 12th to 14th centuries. Greek painters introduced the icon into Russia and the Russian Andrew Roublev (c. 1360–c. 1430) brought the style to a magnificent pitch of development. Crete remained a centre until the 16th century and there is still a trace of the Byzantine tradition in the paintings of El Greco (c. 1545–1614).

EARLY CHRISTIAN ART IN THE WEST

East or west, early Christian art in general avoided the realistic imitation of the human form that had been a feature of classical art. Yet it was not necessarily crude and imperfect, but more spiritual and abstract, in the sense of being removed from mundane affairs; and from this point of view it is nowadays judged more favourably than it used to be. Early Christian art in the west has an intricate history. It followed first the Greco-Roman tradition as in the paintings of the Roman catacombs. It was modified by the local character of the various regions into which the Roman Empire was re-grouped. It was affected by its communications, religious and commercial, with the Eastern Empire. The monastic art of the illuminated manuscripts was for a long time the main form of pictorial art, as in Celtic and Anglo-Saxon Britain and in the empire of Charlemagne. Two things became increasingly clear with time: that Christianity was the one unifying and educational force in Europe, and that pictures were a principal means of conveying its message effectively and universally among people speaking different tongues or unable to read and write. With the great period of church building, from the 11th century, the international western style known as Romanesque developed. Its greatest products were the wall paintings of churches. Working on a large area, the painters developed a bold and simple style of much grandeur.

GOTHIC ART

The monumental Romanesque style was not however of long duration. It disappeared with the radical change in western architecture, the advent of the Gothic church. The increased window space of the lofty cathedral replaced wall painting with the "picture" of stained glass. Sculpture took pride of place as a representational art. Painting was largely confined to the book scale, the illumination of the service and prayer-books, missals and Books of Hours. There was a change, however, in the attitude of the artist (and of his wealthy patrons), a delight in fine detail, gay colour, in human character and the appearance of nature, which had previously been lacking. Its qualities appear in the altarpieces and other works which applied the style of manuscript painting to a larger scale. Altarpieces were executed in tempera, a medium related to the opaque water-colour of the illuminated manuscript, but a new and glorious future for painting came with the development of the oil medium in the 15th century. The paintings of Jan van Eyck (c. 1390–1441), who worked at Bruges, represent the climax of the detailed and beautiful Gothic style and an early perfection of oil painting.

THE RENAISSANCE

In Italy the Gothic style never took a strong hold. Church building was not drastically changed in character as it was in France and England. Artists continued to produce wall-paintings on a large scale and masterpieces were produced in constant succession from the end of the 13th century onwards. At the same time there was a change of outlook which attained its full development in the 16th century and is indicated by the word "Renaissance". Strictly speaking it means "rebirth", and in art it refers to a revived interest in the classic productions of the ancient world. Thus the human figure which the artists of the Middle Ages had shunned once again became the artist's main subject.

This, however, was only one aspect of the Renaissance. It marked the end of the Middle Ages in another way: in the growth of a desire for knowledge and the spirit of science. Artists began to study anatomy and the effects of light and shadow, which made their work more life-like. These studies were practised all the more freely because of a growing taste among the Italian patrons of art for other than religious subjects, for example those taken from classical myth in which the artist could group at his discretion nude and clothed figures, buildings and landscape. Botticelli is one of the great examples.

The heyday of the Renaissance is to be placed between the 15th and 16th centuries in Italy, and its great representatives are Leonardo da Vinci, Michelangelo, Raphael, Giorgione, Titian and Tintoretto. They used the perfected science of painting to create harmonies and rhythms of unsurpassed majesty and beauty.

BAROQUE AND ROCOCO

Two international styles followed the Renaissance. The first is known as Baroque. It is marked by dramatic gesture and movement and was often a sort of imposing propaganda for Church and State. The work of the great Flemish painter Rubens in the 17th century provides an outstanding example of this style. It was followed in the 18th century by Rococo, a graceful and artificial mode of interior decoration, and lighter in style, exemplified for example in the paintings of the French artists, Boucher and Fragonard.

THE NATIONAL SCHOOLS

The observer will note that the foregoing international terms do not refer to painting alone but also to architecture and sculpture and minor forms of art and craftsmanship, such as tapestries and furniture. For a great church or the palace of a king or prince a consistent style was required. It was to some extent independent, at this princely and ecclesiastical level, from differences of race and nationality. Meanwhile, however, these differences, together with growing variations in religious beliefs and types of society, tended to produce national "schools" of art. A "school" implies a number of painters working in the same region whose work has some general likeness of style and outlook. Each of the main countries of Europe has, at one period or another, produced such groups of artists, whose work is not only of outstanding interest but distinct in its regional and national character.

Thus *Italy* is not only the country of the great movement called the Renaissance; it represents also a whole series of schools which grew up in the various city states into which the country was anciently divided—Florence, Siena, Parma, Venice and so on. *Florence* was astonishingly rich in great artists. They include Giotto, Fra Angelico, Botticelli, Leonardo and Michelangelo to mention only a few whose fame is universal. In Florence the "scientific" attitude which enabled the artist to represent convincingly the weight and dignity of form in the round was cultivated to the highest degree. In this sense the Florentine genius may be called sculptural. *Venice* was the centre of another great school—here again there is a long list of famous artists, including Giovanni Bellini, Carpaccio, Giorgione, Titian, Tintoretto, Veronese and in the 18th century, Canaletto and Guardi. The Venetian School is noted for its rich colour and a more sensuous character than that of the intellectual Florentines. In the 16th century *Bologna* was the centre of a school that tried to pick out and combine the best qualities of a number of the earlier masters. Naples in the 17th century was the centre of a rather sombre *Spanish-Italian School* of whom Ribera is typical.

The great period of the Southern Netherlands, the *Flemish School* extends from the 15th to the 17th century, though it has two distinct aspects. There is first the highly detailed and mainly religious art (though including portraiture) of the early masters, van Eyck, van der Weyden and Memlinc (Pl. 14); and secondly the florid and vigorous art, varied in subject matter, which is supremely represented by Rubens (Pl. 12).

The *Dutch School* is the product of one century, the 17th, in which the northern provinces of the Netherlands attained their independence. It is marked by a strongly national feeling and pride in its middle-class prosperity, its well kept interiors, its characteristic flat landscape, its flowers. The Dutch greatly developed portraiture, landscape and still-life and gave to art two of its greatest masters in Rembrandt and Vermeer.

French painting reaches a sustained level from the 17th to the 19th century. Centrally placed between north and south Europe, France was influenced both by Italian and Flemish art, though developing a strong individuality, to be seen in such great masters as Nicolas Poussin and Claude, Watteau, Chardin and Fragonard (Pl. 13). A brilliant succession of painters in the 19th century, from Corot and Delacroix to Manet and the Impressionists, makes this perhaps the most remarkable period of all in French painting.

The great period of *British painting* is from the early 18th to the early 19th century. Beginning with Hogarth and his pictures of social life, it comprises the achievements in portraiture of Gainsborough, Reynolds and others, and in landscape of Wilson, Gainsborough, Crome, Turner and Constable; while its school of water-colour painting was a growth without parallel elsewhere.

German art flowered in the 16th century, combining the Gothic passion for detail with an intense earnestness that did not shrink from ugliness. The great artists of this period are Matthias Grünewald, who added a masterpiece to European painting in his *Isenheim Altarpiece*, and Albrecht Dürer whose engravings and drawings are among the great classics of art.

The genius of *Spain* likewise is concentrated in a

few men of outstanding greatness: El Greco in the late 16th century, Velazquez, who in achievement and influence is one of the greatest of all, and finally Goya with his keen social vision (Pl. 38).

The great social changes of the 19th century profoundly affected the position of the artist and the character of what he produced. There was a new race of patrons, wealthy with the expansion of commerce and industry, and eager to acquire works of art. For the most part, however, they were exclusively interested in an anecdote or story of some kind rather than in the beauty of a picture. Painters who satisfied this need grew wealthy also, but the subject pictures they produced, concerned only with the story, were often worthless as art. A certain number of artists braved unpopularity or neglect to go their own way, in the effort to produce new beauties of form and colour and to raise painting above the trivial level of anecdote. In Britain the Pre-Raphaelites made their heroic effort in the 1850s. In France painters were even more a separate group, enduring poverty and hardship but steadily pursuing their own aims. The movement called Impressionism became the main focus of this effort and in the work of Edouard Manet, Claude Monet, Camille Pissarro, Auguste Renoir and others it produced splendid results. The brilliant draughts-manship of Degas and Toulouse-Lautrec with its vivid impressions of Parisian life is another aspect of this creative age.

Thus the century was one of strange and emphatic contrast. There is a mass of lifeless and bad work which was once popular. There is also a wonderful development of colour and the painting of light and atmosphere which is now properly valued.

Modern painting has grown from this development of the 19th century. The number of movements differently named which mark this process are sometimes confusing to the lay person but it has to be remembered that they show, in much the same way as the enlarged vocabulary of modern science, the amount of thought and energy that has opened up new prospects. The glossary given below, as well as giving brief definitions, is arranged chronologically to show the sequence of ideas from the early 19th century to the present day. It should be added that the emphasis in the last hundred years, not on subject matter or story but on form and colour as a universal language, has enabled us to understand better the art of the East. One of the great discoveries of the 19th century was the Japanese colour print which opened the eyes of European artists to the value of selection and concentration on the essentials both of colour and form.

FORMS OF ART
IN THE 19TH AND 20TH CENTURIES

Classicism. In painting, the work of those who attached the main importance to composition, figure painting and figure drawing, and were influenced in some degree by the ideal character of "classical"—i.e., Greek or Greco-Roman figure sculpture. It took a special form as a return to the antique with the French painter J. L. David (1748–1825) and later with J. A. D. Ingres (1780–1867).

Romanticism. A tendency opposed to classicism, laying stress on personal and emotional expression, especially in colour and dramatic effect. It appeared in the early 19th century in varying forms in Britain, France and Germany. The landscapes of Turner (1775–1851) show its influence on British painting and those of Caspar David Friedrich (1774–1840) reflect the trend in Germany. The outstanding French romantics were Théodore Géricault (1791–1824) and Eugène Delacroix (1796–1863).

Realism was the product of the 1840s and was an effort to depict life and nature as they really were, rejecting the fanciful subjects and artificial mannerisms of style that belonged to the past—it was called by Gustave Courbet "democratic art". Courbet (1819–1877) was a leader of Realism in France and in its beginning the English Pre-Raphaelite movement (1848) had a similar intention in its aim of "truth to Nature".

Pre-Raphaelitism. The Pre-Raphaelite Brotherhood, founded by D. G. Rossetti, J. E. Millais and W. Holman Hunt in 1848 comprised several aims, one being realism (Pl. 15). It was also an effort to purify art by returning to the earnest spirit of early Italian painting before Raphael. It was very influential, though its effect was somewhat confused by its mixture of ideas.

Impressionism. This beautiful phase of painting

followed Realism, developing c. 1860–1870 and reaching its maturity after the Franco-Prussian War, c. 1870–1880. It added to the Realist aim of painting everyday life and landscape the effort to convey the truth of atmospheric effect, using a technique which translated light and shade into definite colour, abolishing the dingy blacks and browns that were then common. Famous painters connected with it are Edouard Manet, Claude Monet, Camille Pisarro, Auguste Renoir, Edgar Degas. Its influence in Britain is seen in the work of Philip Wilson Steer and Walter Richard Sickert.

Pointillism. An extension of the Impressionist method, entailing the scientific combination of the primary colours, red, yellow and blue, in a mosaic of dots or patches, fusing when seen at a distance into various tones, but giving a heightened and vibrating effect. Georges Seurat (1859–1891) and Paul Signac were the practitioners of this method, a main result of which was to encourage the use of brilliant colour.

Post-Impressionism. This term refers not to one style, but to the painters who followed in the wake of Impressionism and modified it in various ways, either to give more firmness of structure or more of a personal character. Thus the French painter Paul Cézanne (1839–1906) sought to express solid form by noting the different colour produced by light on each plane of a rounded or other three-dimensional shape. Paul Gauguin (1848–1903) in his paintings of the South Sea Island natives simplified form in the earlier style of the mural painters (Pl. 16). The Dutch artist Vincent van Gogh (1853–1890) gives a personal and highly emotional character to methods learned from Pissarro and Seurat. A local school in Britain influenced by this phase of art was the Camden Town Group (Spencer Gore, R. Bevan, H. Gilman, C. Ginner and others) who produced delightful work.

Fauvism. About 1905 a group of painters in France, headed by Henri Matisse, were called *les fauves* (wild beasts) because they used colour with an apparent wildness. The aim of Fauvism was to exploit the value of colour in itself, quite apart from natural effect.

Cubism. A movement of much influence which developed between 1907 and 1914 and became merged with other ideas in the first post-war period. It began as an effort to bring out the geometric structure of objects (following the theory of Cézanne). As a result, the idea of structure (like the colour of the Fauvists) was separated from the old realism, though the Cubist still-life makes free use of familiar objects to compose a decorative pattern or arrangement of forms. The living artists Pablo Picasso and Georges Braque were its originators. One influence of Cubism may be seen in the bold and decided character of some 20th century posters.

Futurism. Stemming from Cubism, c. 1912, was the aggressive Italian movement called Futurism, launched by the poet Marinetti. It sought to interpret the spirit of the 20th century in terms of movement, speed and machine forms. *Vorticism* in Britain, in which the artist and writer P. Wyndham Lewis played a large part, owed something both to

Cubism and Futurism as an attempt to express the character of the age.

Expressionism. In Germany and Austria, the underlying desire already noted in other countries for a new art expressive of the 20th century is somewhat vaguely described as Expressionism. It was based on the idea that the business of the artist is not to produce an illusion of reality, but to convey something of the artist himself and his feelings. The Norwegian artist Edvard Munch and Vincent van Gogh helped to inspire its violent character. Emil Nolde (b. 1867), Wassily Kandinsky (b. 1866) and Oskar Kokoschkas (b. 1886) represent various aspects of the movement.

Surrealism. In the decade before the Second World War, Surrealism grew up as an effort to show, through painting and drawing, the workings of pure instinct and the subconscious mind, and also to interpret that dream world which psycho-analysis had explored. It demonstrated that art can gain a powerful stimulus from the free exercise of the imagination. Imaginative art, more or less related to Surrealism, is that of the Italian Giorgio di Chirico, the Swiss Paul Klee, the Spaniard Salvador Dali, and the British painter Graham Sutherland.

Abstract Art. The effort to gain an effect akin to that of music without imitation of natural forms. To some extent it was an offshoot of Cubism and made use of geometrical systems of form in its earlier phases, though latterly it has made some use of the random patterns to be found in nature. It relies greatly on the appeal of colour.

PART FOUR

The Artist's Theme

CHAPTER I

LANDSCAPE

LANDSCAPE, it is clear, is one of the principal means by which artists express their delight in the visible world, though as one of the great departments of art it is a comparatively modern growth. Primitive peoples did not practise it—the forests and jungles around them, full of unknown terrors, had no special meaning for them such as the record of hunting and battle possessed. Landscape was introduced into painting when man gained some measure of control over nature. For a long time it was simply the background for pictures of human beings, and there are few masterpieces of the art that do not introduce some feature that tells of human presence and activity.

Nature first appears in the form of clearly defined objects: thus in Egyptian wall-painting we see the papyrus plants of the Nile delta, each plant carefully outlined. Water, obviously a more difficult problem, is rendered by a sort of shorthand or symbolism in a series of wavy lines. For long ages thereafter, landscape was treated in an elementary way (though the Greek painters had some idea of space and there are scenes illustrating the Odyssey, now in the Vatican, which show a perspective of rocks and a distant horizon). It is not, however, until towards the end of our Middle Ages that Nature begins to have a really important part in painting. Thus the changes of the seasons and the human activity that goes with each are beautifully seen in the paintings of a famous Book of Hours, the *Très Riches Heures du Duc de Berry* (Musée Condé, Chantilly) at the beginning of the 15th century. In this painted calendar, for instance, we see a merry cavalcade in the month of May, riding through the fresh greenery and among the spring flowers.

Landscape as a background is often delightful in the work of Flemish and Italian painters principally noted for their figure compositions. We get fascinating glimpses of little towns, winding rivers and stretches of wooded country, and it is a pleasant exercise for the observer to walk round one of the great art galleries and pick out these details. Then there are pictures where the setting is a dramatic part of the main theme: the snow-covered landscape intensifies the force of Pieter Brueghel the Elder's *Census of Bethlehem* (Brussels). The mountain distance of Titian's *Bacchus and Ariadne* (National Gallery) adds to the incomparable spirit and vigour of this picture. Yet the first pictures in which landscape took pride of place were those of travellers from northern Europe to Italy (the centre of art) whose eyes were opened to unfamiliar scenes and places of interest. Thus Dürer has left a remarkable series of landscape water-colours from his southward journey. In the later 17th century northern artists working in Rome (e.g. the Fleming Paul Bril, the German Adam Elsheimer) produced pictures in which landscape was the main interest. A vogue grew up for views of Rome and its environs associated with classical antiquity.

Of this "classical landscape", Claude of Lorraine (1600–1682) is superbly representative. His achievement was twofold. He was the first to represent the spaciousness and radiance of the sky and to bathe the whole of a landscape in its glow. Dawn and sunset were his favourite times of day and two great pictures in the National Gallery, the *Embarkation of the Queen of Sheba* and the *Embarkation of St. Ursula*, show him at his best in rendering the glow of evening. The fanciful figures and buildings are of less importance than the sun against which the rigging and crow's-nests of the 17th-century ship is outlined; and which tips the waves with golden light and sparkles on trees and imaginative palaces (Pl. 18).

Another side of Claude's genius is seen in his drawings of the Campagna and the hill country round Rome. These, executed with a pen line and a warm monochrome, show the realistic observer seizing on the essential facts of natural form. A tree to Giotto, for instance, is a selection of leaves and branches precisely outlined. Claude shows how foliage can be summed up as a mass, or solid form, denoted by light and shade.

In the 17th century other great artists turned to landscape for various reasons. Rubens gives us a great masterpiece in his picture of his own house and the surrounding country, the *Château de Steen* (National Gallery). It is panoramic, like the work of the earlier 16th-century Fleming Patenier, but Rubens with greater power employs both the most minute and the most general observation. One notices the light sparkling in the windows of the mansion, the spreading distance; how the foreground is enlivened by a wealth of incident, the farm waggon and the sportsman with his gun after partridge. Here the artist is painting the part of his homeland he knows and loves best (Pl. 19). He is also painting light and space, and these subsequently are the main factors in the development of landscape in the Netherlands, Britain and France.

Thus the Dutch painters of the 17th century delight in their neat and well-cultivated country. They are the first to give a complete "portrait" of their own land. Hobbema's masterpiece *The Avenue at Middelharnis* (National Gallery) with its formal row of lopped trees leading the eye into the picture and its trim patches of kitchen garden, is one aspect of it (Pl. 18). At the same time the flat land and low horizon led the artists to study the expanse of sky, the clouds and the cloud shadows on the flat land. This is beautifully seen in works by Philips, Koninck and some by Jacob van Ruysdael. In a great number of drawings and etchings, Rembrandt conveys the homely attraction of canals, windmills and little clumps of trees. Jan Vermeer produces one of the world's great pictures in his *View of Delft* (Hague) where the interesting silhouette of the town, the reflections in the water, the figures on the quay are placed so unerringly in relation to one another that nothing could well be altered—there is endless pleasure for the eye in this perfect balance (Pl. 20).

British artists in the 18th century were influenced to some extent by the "classical landscape" produced in Italy but still more by the Dutch. In oil painting Richard Wilson (1714–1782) comes first. He worked in Rome and there is something of Claude in his glowing skies. His art is noted for what is called "breadth", that is, for simplifying forms into certain main shapes which sum up the essentials of a scene. Many of his best landscapes are views along the Thames or in Wales.

It was in East Anglia, however, country which had some affinity to the landscape of Holland, that British landscape painting flourished most typically. The "Norwich School", a local group of Norfolk artists headed by John Crome (1768–1821), is famous, though he is by far its greatest personality. A magnificent picture is his *Mousehold Heath* (Victoria and Albert Museum). It depicts a shepherd-boy and his dog with a few sheep on a piece of broken, tufted ground. There is nothing of unusual interest in the subject matter: what makes it good is the sense of vast space created by the boy's silhouette against the sky: the art which collects the simple elements of which the picture

60

is composed and binds them together into a strong design.

Thomas Gainsborough (1727–1788) had a love of his native Suffolk which gave him a life-long preference for landscape painting rather than the portraits which made him successful. He shows us two aspects of the art: first in his early works views that are as typically English as those of Ruysdael are typically Dutch, like his *Wood Scene, Cornard* with its sturdy oaks (National Gallery); secondly, in the days of his fame and city life, he painted country scenes from imagination in which the play of light among masses of foliage is more closely studied than the character of any particular tree. A famous example is *The Market Cart*, and though the trees and the place have no reality, the picture attains one of the great ends of landscape painting in being full of light.

The rise of water-colour landscape was a separate development. It was encouraged by the demand in the later 18th century for drawings of places and buildings of historic interest which could be engraved and used as illustrations for books. The portable water-colour equipment was suitable for artists who now travelled about Britain, recording landscape as well as buildings, in Wales, Scotland and Yorkshire as well as in the south. Paul Sandby (1725–1809) was one of the first. Some artists extended their travels abroad, accompanying men of wealth on their Grand Tour to Italy. J. R. Cozens (1752–1799) was one of the best. The water-colourists acquired a great dexterity with the brush which is sometimes compared with that of Far Eastern painters. John Sell Cotman (1782–1842) gives an example. Their swift washes of light colour lent themselves to the notation of atmospheric effect. The great artist who emerged from this school was J. M. W. Turner (1775–1851).

Turner left a vast mass of work, oil paintings, water-colours and drawings. A great traveller and keen observer, he was equally at home on land and sea, and the list of his masterpieces is long and varied. It includes his *Calais Pier*, a wonderfully vigorous study of rough sea, *Frosty Morning*, in which the crisp atmosphere is conveyed in a design of beautiful simplicity, and the splendid blaze of colour in his *Ulysses deriding Polyphemus* (Pl. 32). In addition to such oil paintings his water-colours, sometimes executed on toned paper with the addition of opaque white, range from careful topography to the colour-poems of his later years. In these he attains a unique quality.

His contemporary, John Constable (1776–1837), confined himself to English landscape and, like Gainsborough, had a strong affection for his native Suffolk. He was essentially an oil painter, though impressed by the water-colours of Turner's friend Thomas Girtin. It was Constable's achievement to interpret the transient effects of light and atmosphere by broken touches of colour which gave a sparkle and freshness none had ever reached before. A masterpiece is the *Haywain* (National Gallery), first exhibited in 1821, which came as a revelation to French artists when shown at the Salon in 1824.

Also in the National Gallery is his well-known *Cornfield* (Pl. 17). The large sketches by Constable for this or for his *Leaping Horse* show the sparkling freedom of his technique.

After Constable and Turner, the great development of landscape painting was in France. J. B. C. Corot became its great representative (1796–1875). Early pictures of Rome and the South of France suggest the influence of Constable, but he is better known for pictures of a silvery grey tone, in which the breeze seems to ripple through delicate foliage. He was revered by the younger generation which produced Impressionist landscapes. Between 1860 and 1870 a group led by Claude Monet (1840–1926), working on the outskirts of Paris and in Normandy in the open air (like the English water-colourists), brought a new element into landscape by translating light into terms of pure colour (Pl. 23). Today Impressionist landscape is especially valued for the fresh and brilliant effect thus obtained. French landscape reached its final height in the work of Paul Cézanne (1839–1906). His *Mont Ste. Victoire* (Tate Gallery) is a great picture in which colour builds up the essential structure of the scene. Vincent van Gogh (1853–1890) shows an intense personal feeling in his pictures of the landscape round Arles which makes them lastingly memorable.

CHAPTER II

IMAGINATIVE
SUBJECT COMPOSITION

THE first paintings that may be included under this heading are murals discovered at Pompeii, Roman copies of the 1st century A.D. of earlier works. They show how the ancient world had already devised a type of subject picture, based on their myths and legends, and allowing the artist freedom to represent dramatic effects of movement, expression and light and shade, and to compose figures, architecture and even landscape in some ordered grouping.

In the time of the Italian Renaissance, when the artist was no longer strictly confined to religious painting, there was some return to this ancient subject matter: the classic myths and stories once again gave their challenge to the artist's imagination. "Imagination" implied some ideal conception in which the painter was not bound by fact: his human gods and goddesses, clothed in draperies which belonged to no historic period, or unclothed, moved freely in space and in timeless settings, and magnificent rhythms were the result.

Fables, allegories (that is, pictures in which ideas were personified) and scenes relating to the ancient world, in which the question of historical accuracy did not arise, have produced some of the

17. JOHN CONSTABLE
The Cornfield

MEINDERT HOBBEMA: *The Avenue, Middelharnis*

18.   CLAUDE: *Harbour at Sunset*

19. PETER PAUL RUBENS
Autumn: The Château de Steen

20. JAN VERMEER
View of Delft

21. TITIAN
Bacchus and Ariadne

22.   THOMAS GIRTIN: *Durham Cathedral and Bridge* (water-colour)

Collection H. H. Levy, Esq.

23. CLAUDE MONET: *Waterloo Bridge*

24. PIERO DELLA FRANCESCA
Detail from *The Nativity*

Convent of San Marco, Florence

25. FRA ANGELICO
The Annunciation

26. MATTHIAS GRÜNEWALD
The Crucifixion

27. ALBRECHT DÜRER
Knight, Death and the Devil
(line engraving)

28. Tintoretto
The Origin of the Milky Way

National Gallery, London

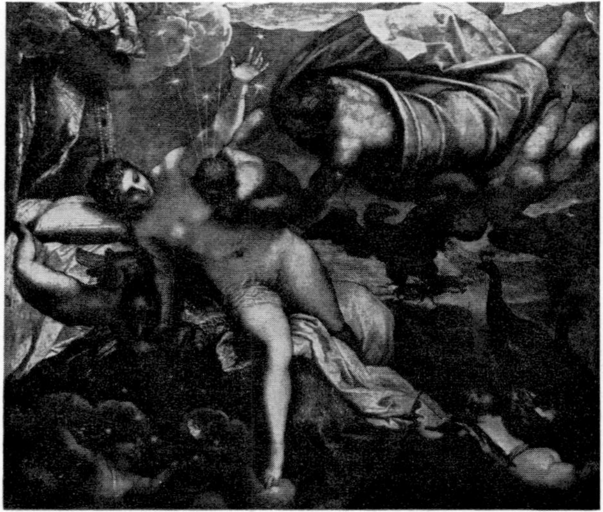

29.   BOTTICELLI: *The Birth of Venus*

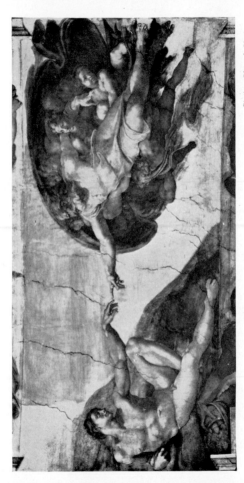

30. MICHELANGELO: *The Creation of Adam*

Sistine Chapel, Vatican

31.   WILLIAM BLAKE: "*Pity, like a newborn babe*"

32. J. M. W. TURNER
Ulysses deriding Polyphemus

greatest European pictures. Titian's masterpiece *Bacchus and Ariadne* is a famous example (Pl. 21). The fable is that of Ariadne, deserted in Naxos by Theseus, startled from her melancholy by the advent of the young, handsome Bacchus and his gay crew. Yet one can appreciate this marvellous work without knowing the story. The contrasting movements of Ariadne and the young Bacchus leaping from his chariot impart a tremendous buoyancy and lightness of feeling. This is combined with and enhanced by the rich contrast of Ariadne's blue cloak and Bacchus's crimson draperies. While the general plan of form and colour is so bold, the subject gives Titian freedom to introduce a multitude of beautiful details: a splendid landscape distance, animals with beautiful coats, a sly little faun in whose hair the artist has minutely painted a white flower. Well known as it is, this is a picture one can go back to again and again, without coming to the end of its fascination. Among allegories one may single out *Venus, Cupid, Folly and Time* by the Florentine Bronzino (1503–1572). Venus, who holds the apple of discord, is embraced by Cupid, while Folly, a laughing cherub, throws flowers at her and a stern Time stretches out his arm. The rhythm consists in the fashion in which one form seems to catch up and repeat that of another while the horizontal of Time's arm brings its uncompromising barrier in contrast with the soft and yielding figures of the foreground.

Another Italian masterpiece, by a greater man than Bronzino, is *The Origin of the Milky Way* by

Tintoretto (1518–1594). It is a fanciful subject that an artist could interpret in a number of ways. The Venetian master shows Jove placing the infant Hercules at Juno's breasts—fountains which produce a starry galaxy (Pl. 28). The wonderful thing about the picture, however, is not this playful symbolism but the majestic movement and the power with which these rounded forms are completely realized in space. One can look on it as an intricate balance of forces resolved with great skill, though the charm of Juno remains the human focus of interest.

Italy, indeed, more than any country, has given us a wealth of great pictures based on such general themes which allow free rein to the artist's invention. The *Primavera* of Botticelli (1445–1510), an allegory of the seasons, weaves various symbolic figures—the Three Graces, Flora, Mercury—into a design, the effect of which is like visual music. *The School of Athens*, one of Raphael's frescoes in the Vatican, takes Philosophy as its theme. This is rendered in a mighty composition in which all the science and spirit of the Renaissance is grandly displayed. The long perspective of arches, the setting of a number of figures in space, the expressiveness and variety of gesture, equally command admiration. It was work of this kind on which Sir Joshua Reynolds based his analysis of the "Grand Style" as the loftiest form of painting.

As one travels westward and northward in Europe, one finds a different kind of imaginative composition. Rubens, it is true, gives us allegory inspired by his study of Italian art. A splendid example is *Peace and War* in the National Gallery, in which we see figures representing Wealth and Happiness, and Minerva repelling War; though the artist's interest is concentrated not so much on grandeur of rhythm as on the richness of material textures, the warmth of flesh tones, and the abundance of fruits, all are painted with marvellous skill (Pl. 12). In France, Nicolas Poussin (1594–1655) paints pictures of Bacchanalian festival, dance and other themes that reflect an imaginary antique world. As with the Renaissance Italians whose work he studied, his aim is what one can only call "nobility of composition", the selection of essentials of mass, grouping, expressive gesture, and light and shade. Sometimes his vision of antiquity seems formal and scholarly rather than full of imaginative life.

On the whole as one goes away from Italy the classic past loses its spell and imaginative composition takes a quite different form, satirical, mysterious, melancholy or weird; while if it is inspired by the past it is by the Gothic past of northern Europe rather than the Mediterranean world. Thus in two masterpieces of graphic art, Albrecht Dürer strikes the note of sombre contemplation. In his famous engraving *Melancolia*, the figure of Humanity broods sadly over its imperfect achievements. In his *Knight, Death and the Devil* the armoured figure on his way is ever accompanied by the two nagging and ghastly images (Pl. 27). A weirdly satirical imagination is to be seen in the work of the Netherlandish painter Hieronymus

Bosch (1462–1516). Ostensibly his subjects are religious, but a weird and satirical element predominates and possesses a fascination which has been strongly felt in modern times. His greatest work is the so-called *Garden of Terrestrial Delights*, which is in the Prado Gallery, Madrid. It is in three parts: on the one side is the Garden of Eden, in the centre the World, with a vast number of figures which one can take as symbolizing worldly pleasures, and finally an extraordinary vision of an inferno, with blazing ruins in the background and the strangest medley of goblins and human, animal and vegetable forms in the foreground. It contains a whole language of symbols, some of which are mysterious, and some ingenious attempts have been made to interpret them and relate them to the psycho-analytic study of symbols and dreams. Whatever one makes of them there is no doubt of the artist's amazing powers of invention.

There exists some difference of opinion as to the value of this kind of imagination in pictorial art. Some critics, like Roger Fry, have held that it detracts from the beauty of form and colour which should exist, and be appreciated, in itself and that it is not therefore "pure art". On the other hand it is clear that art allows of many different ways of expression, and that completeness and power of expression create their own special beauty which is independent of any fixed system of appraisal. Thus the work of the remarkable English poet and designer William Blake (1757–1827) is complete and powerful as the product of a singularly gifted mind, though we cannot compare it with that of the great Italian masters as a rendering of physical substance. Blake despised the imitation of nature or material qualities. What he tries to convey is the inward vision (Pl. 31). In his great engravings to the *Book of Job* he takes us into a world that is not material but belongs only to the mind: in the famous engraving of the *Morning Stars* his spiritual feeling is perfectly expressed in a wonderful design.

Imaginative art indeed takes many forms. With the great Spanish artist Goya (1746–1828) it becomes fiercely satirical. Through his etched *Caprices* he attacked the follies and vices of his time, and though the meaning is obscure to us the strange force of his imagination is to be felt in every incisive line. There is a painting by him, *The Prison*, in which his sense of horror at human confinement and misery is given emphasis by a sombre arch and the dim light that filters through it on to a group of huddled figures.

Literature too has had its inspiration to give: Homer, Dante, Shakespeare and Milton have provided the artist with many subjects. Twentieth century criticism has been suspicious of this tendency on the ground that the spectators' attention is diverted to the story or literary theme and away from the qualities of form and colour; and this is certainly a flaw in some 19th-century pictures. On the other hand, there are many instances when the imagination of the artist is encouraged to add something to the theme. The beautiful fresco by the Umbrian painter Pinturicchio of *The Return of*

Odysseus (National Gallery) gives a delightful version of the scene from Homer in the costume of the painter's own time. William Blake's water-colour drawings of Dante's *Divine Comedy* (Tate Gallery) are a pictorial poem of colour and movement. The Anglo-Swiss painter Henry Fuseli who depicted the court of Oberon and Titania from *A Midsummer Night's Dream*, devised his own fairy-land full of curious elves and gnomes.

It is a function of imaginative art to transport us from the everyday world to life and landscape conceived in the mind, and more recent painting is not without its examples. An instance is provided by the French painter Henri Rousseau (1844–1910), popularly known as the *Douanier* or "Customs House Officer" from the minor official post he long occupied. Haunted by a vague memory of tropical America (seen during a period of military service), Rousseau devised pictures of the jungle, in which palm-fronds, fruits, animals and figures are sharply outlined in a way that is sometimes called quaint or primitive, though they constitute a sort of exotic dreamland full of fascination.

Modern imaginative composition is most strikingly represented by works inspired by the Surrealist movement. Here the strangeness of dreams and the mixture of images they call up is deliberately made a feature of the painting. A precursor of surrealism was the living Italian painter Giorgio di Chirico, whose mysterious arcades and perspectives with their warning shadows and decayed statues well create the dream atmosphere. The Catalonian artist

Salvador Dali has exploited the conception of a plain, endlessly receding, in which the mind seems to wander, meeting with surprising objects as in a nightmare: and it is interesting to note the influence of this on the presentation of fantastic ballet sequences in some American films.

An imaginative view of nature, with its remarkable accidents and vagaries of rock and tree forms, was another product of surrealism. Thus some artists have found in close-ups of natural detail a new revelation of the wonder of nature. The work of Paul Nash and Graham Sutherland in Britain has provided striking instances. Painters in the past, for instance Gainsborough, have been able to construct mountains, lakes and woods from the suggestion offered by pebbles, bits of moss and a small puddle. There is the same basic idea that the magic of form is present in all things and in wonderful variety.

CHAPTER III

THE RELIGIOUS SUBJECT

THE purpose of religious painting in Europe has been twofold. Its first object was to present in visible form the conception of eternal and unchanging truth. In the earlier phase of the Christian era up to and including the period known as Romanesque, A.D. c. 1100, we find a formal style of art, with fixed conventions, which stood for this unchanging character. It appears both in illuminated manuscripts and in the wall paintings of churches and is most notable in Byzantine work, where the icon endlessly repeats the same formula. This is not necessarily a crude art as the casual observer might think, but has the value of a strict discipline in its exclusion of human interest which often gives a spiritual grandeur of its own.

The second purpose was that of presenting to the masses the central episodes of the New Testament story. In the course of time it became clear that these could effectively be presented in a number of ways which brought home to the spectator their essential and universal humanity. The theme of Mother and Child is one great example. Artists were able to depict different types, costumes and settings according to their time and place of work, without failing in reverence, and indeed they conveyed the eternal no less truthfully by clothing it in this changing and human guise. In the same way the Crucifixion could be treated in many ways without losing the essential idea of sacrifice to a great end. So we find, from the Gothic period onwards in the north and from the 13th century onwards in Italy, that these two themes are constantly repeated and yet always offer us some new aspect of conception and style; and that these latter vary, far more than in early Christian art, with the personality or the nationality of the artist. They are not, of course, the only themes. The Creation, the Fall, the Last Judgement, the triumph of

Christianity in the form of an "Adoration", the deeds of the Apostles, the lives of the saints, and Old Testament history in various narrative aspects, are among the religious themes which occupied many of the greatest European artists for some five hundred years.

We may take as representative of the northern or Gothic spirit in religious art two masterpieces, one Flemish and one German: the *Adoration of the Lamb* (Ghent Cathedral), ascribed by tradition to the two brothers Hubert and Jan van Eyck, and the *Isenheim Altarpiece* (Colnar Museum) by Matthias Grünewald. The former has all that interest in rich and varied detail and incident that is typical of early Flemish art and forms a kind of pictorial hymn of praise. God, with the Madonna and St. John the Baptist on either side, singing angels and Adam and Eve, occupy an upper row of panels: below is the most beautiful part of the altarpiece in which the Holy Ghost and Christ, represented by the symbols of the Dove and the Lamb, are set in the middle of an idyllic parkland, surrounded by a host of worshippers. The smooth brilliance of technique, and the minute detail which distinguishes each figure as a human personality, show the happy interest of the artists in the life around them and the superb craftsmanship with which they were able to render it.

Yet it is sometimes said of Christian art that it first introduced the idea of suffering, and it is the feeling of tragedy and pain that we get from the work of Grünewald, very different from the product of the prosperous and contented Netherlands (Pl. 26). The series of folding panels of the Isenheim altarpiece are a sort of tragic symphony. Cruelty and pain are conveyed in the sombrely intense colour and tortured forms of the Crucifixion seen when the panels are closed. The most sinister of landscapes and nightmare creatures appear in the subsidiary panels of the Temptation of St. Anthony. Yet this is a work which shows that a picture need not be pretty to be beautiful, and that its sombre intensity is raised to beauty by the completeness of the artist's power and vision.

In Italy a long succession of painters working mainly in fresco on the walls of monasteries and churches gave to the religious theme both grandeur and humanity. The Florentine Giotto (1267–1337), contemporary of Dante who praised his work, is the first great example. His principal works are the frescoes depicting the Life of St. Francis at Assisi and those devoted to the Life of Christ in the Arena Chapel, Padua. In them he gives a quality of relief and natural expression together with an emphasis on the main features of the action represented that inspired all his successors. A similar dignified simplicity appears in Fra Angelico (1387–1455) though accompanied by a gentler feeling for colour and gracefulness of posture as in his *Annunciation* at Florence (Pl. 25). Another Florentine, Masaccio (1401–1428), goes further than Giotto in giving rounded substance to his figures, with something of a sculptor's sense of plastic form. As we come nearer to the fully developed Italian Renaissance of the 15th to 16th centuries we see how the various researches of the Italian painters in perspective, anatomy and light and shade, together with a conception of ideal human beauty, all come together with overwhelming effect in religious art. One can only mention here Andrea Castagno (1423–1457), Filippo Lippi (1406–1469), Ghirlandaio (1449–1494), Signorelli (c. 1441–1523), but we must pause before the greatness of Piero della Francesca (?1416–1492). A man of scientific mind, he worked out his compositions with geometrical precision, but this is harmonized with a graciousness of type and gesture that can be well appreciated in the masterpieces in the National Gallery, more particularly his *Nativity* (Pl. 24). It may be compared with the same subject as treated in another great picture, also in the National Gallery, by Botticelli (c. 1444–1510), to which a ring of fluttering angels gives a joyous movement.

In the great religious paintings at the height of the Renaissance we notice the absence of the simple devotional feeling of a Fra Angelico. They are something more than, or different from, paintings for the Church, but are profound expressions of human thought, combined with an extraordinary mastery of craft. Leonardo da Vinci's contemporaries marvelled at the way in which the character of the disciples was revealed in his *Last Supper*, though it is now difficult to picture this sadly decayed fresco in its original state. His *Madonna of the Rocks* (National Gallery), however, fully conveys a mysterious and timeless beauty, and the strange landscape background, with its primeval rocks, suggests the antiquity and mystery of life on earth (Pl. 50). In contrast Michelangelo, in the great ceiling and wall-paintings of the Vatican, gives a tremendous epic character to the whole story of humanity. In the *Creation of Adam* (Pl. 30) the life-force seems to flow along the outstretched arm into the still languid body of the newly shaped man. In the *Last Judgement* the turbulent and crowded composition suggests all humanity's conflicts, struggles and failures.

Italian religious painting after Michelangelo's time—and even in his time—was beginning to overlay its ostensible subject with displays of pictorial skill, or with a palpably greater interest in the material rather than the spiritual world, though this did not prevent the production of masterpieces of pictorial rhythm and design. The immense movement in space of innumerable figures in the *Paradise* of Tintoretto (1518–1594) in the Doges' Palace, Venice, is dazzling in its majestic effect. Another Venetian masterpiece is the *Marriage at Cana* (Louvre) by Veronese (1528–1588) in which the eye is diverted by more than a hundred figures, many of them portraits, in the rich dress of Veronese's time. One loses sight of the religious origin of the theme, though the verve of composition and the painting of rich material textures command the utmost admiration and there are probably few pictures in the Louvre that French artists have studied with more respect.

In the 16th and 17th centuries we see in painting

the results of the divergence in religion itself between Catholic and Protestant ideas. The Reformation and the various types of nonconformity connected with it put an end to painting for the Church, in Holland and England in particular. On the other hand, in the Catholic countries, painting was allied with the efforts of the counter-Reformation. The Cretan-Spanish artist known as El Greco (1541–1614) expresses with a wonderful intensity the spiritual fervour that belonged to his adopted country. His *Burial of Count Orgaz* (Toledo Cathedral) with its vision of heavenly forms above and its solemn interment below is one of the greatest of the world's pictures (Pl. 39). In Rubens, however, who represents in religious art the Catholic Southern Netherlands, the painting of the Crucifixion or of miracles is a sort of robust propaganda in which we do not find the best of his wonderful art but a theatricality which has led some critics to complain of his lack of spiritual feeling. With some relief one may turn from it to the cool puritanism of the emancipated northern provinces

The greatest Dutch artist, Rembrandt, it is true, painted and etched many religious subjects, but two great differences between them and the earlier types of this art may be noted. He worked not for a church but as a layman. Secondly, whether he took his subjects from the Old or the New Testament, he always conveys their human aspect. His Apostles are those stately bearded men whom he saw in the Jewish quarter of Amsterdam. His Christ is the man of luminous intelligence, moving in the dusk of human ignorance and doubt. One may analyse separately the extraordinary power of light and shade he gives to his sublime stage, yet technique and human feeling are here marvellously combined.

It is sad to contemplate the sorry images which have been employed in modern times, as far as they have been used at all in the service of any Church. Art has gone its own way, and for some people has become a religion in itself. The sceptical 18th century produced no religious art, except at its end the personal spiritual vision of a William Blake. The 19th century found painters without religious denomination perplexed between their personal religious feelings and the materialistic realism typical of art in their age. Thus the *Light of the World* by Holman Hunt (of which there are versions in Keble College, Oxford and St. Paul's Cathedral in London) is in no way a painting for a church or place of religious devotion, in spite of its earnestness and sincerity. The same might be said of the paintings of Stanley Spencer, whose *Resurrection* is similarly a personal expression of thought. These are pictures which belong to museums rather than to established places of worship. That is not to say that a religious sentiment has died in painters; but the discipline of, and the demand for, their efforts belongs to the past. A modern painter such as Georges Rouault can express the feeling of Christian faith and suffering with a rough sincerity, yet, oddly enough, the art of the present day which is perhaps nearest in spirit to the religious Middle Ages is that known as "abstract". Here there is a rejection of mundane attractions which might have been appreciated by the monkish artists of Winchester in the 14th century.

CHAPTER IV

GENRE PAINTING

GENRE may be defined in dictionary terms as "A style of painting which depicts the scenes and types of common life". It is thus at the opposite extreme from the art concerned with tragic or lofty themes, and is usually associated with comedy, or, in the broadest sense, the "human comedy", with all the social implications of that phrase. As it deals with "low life", the tendency has been to regard it as a lower form of art and to consider its lively picture of modes and manners inferior to the great rhythms and harmonies of form and colour which embody religious and imaginative thought. Yet this, like many other questions of art, cannot be satisfactorily settled in general terms. It is the quality of the individual artist and the truthfulness of his observation and ideas that count. Perhaps the first great painter of genre is the Flemish artist Pieter Brueghel the Elder (c. 1520–1569), and though in almost every respect his art is different from that of the great Italians, it is so original, and so well expresses a national genius, that he may be ranked with the greatest. Two masterpieces at Vienna, the *Village Wedding* (Pl. 34) and the *Peasant Dance* bring the country life of his time before us with amazing vividness. His peasants, coarsely plump or lean and gnarled, are observed perhaps with an amused interest, but without either idealization or caricature. They dance clumsily, drink copiously from earthenware crocks, bring in loads of viands for the feast, quarrel and argue at roughly fashioned tables, play on bagpipes, and each of the many groups is depicted in gesture and character with an unerring sense of real life. Yet we notice also that this multitude of figures is so perfectly arranged and controlled that no detail is lost or confused. While we are aware of the figures we are also aware of the art with which the thatched cottages and trees in the background are painted, and of the sparkling and exciting colour, the favoured Flemish opposition of vermilion red and sage green, the vivid notes of white in headdress, apron or stocking, or touches of black, standing out here and there, against the general light but warm tone.

The peasant life of Flanders inspired further brilliant examples of genre in the 17th century, such as are to be found in the work of David Teniers (1610–1690) and of Adrian Brouwer (1605–1638). Both depict peasants and soldiers revelling, card-playing and blowing clouds of smoke from their pipes in squalid alehouses. Drabness of colour seems deliberately intended to emphasize the sordid character of the scenes, but these painters do not repel us. They have set themselves the aim of depicting the human animal and they pursue it with an almost scientific veracity.

Peasant life in 17th-century France is brilliantly interpreted by the brothers Le Nain, Antoine, Louis and Mathieu, among whom Louis stands out as one of the great French artists of his age (Pl. 36). His little groups of country labourers, despised at that time almost as slaves or subhuman creatures, are depicted not only with sympathetic humanity but with a handling of form that adds a sort of grandeur to the ragged and rough figures of his models. *Saying Grace* (National Gallery) has that element of story or incident which distinguishes genre from group portraiture.

In Holland we ascend in the social scale: the genre picture is of middle-class life, for the most part of a rather grave and static character (Pls. 33 and 37). The company relaxing over a glass of wine in a neatly kept and spacious interior, as depicted by Pieter de Hooch, is not closely characterized, and the interest of such pictures is so much bound up with the effect of space and lighting that genre scarcely seems the right title for them. Genre is perhaps best represented by Jan Steen (1626–1679). In his pictures a middle class, not of the highest pretensions, is observed in its pleasures and humours, and in a gay and light-hearted mood. In theory we should disapprove of the trivial and anecdotal interest—he introduces in a laughing spirit tipsy young women, domestic animals plundering the table and so on—and indeed, in painting, this kind of humour can become intolerable;

yet the resource of composition, the colour, the personal style of Jan Steen are so admirable that he carries it off perfectly.

British artists were evidently much influenced by the Flemish and Dutch pictures of social life. It was left to Hogarth (1697–1764), however, to widen their scope so as to give a complete cross-section of society rather than a study of any one class. He achieved this in the famous series, painted and engraved, the *Harlot's Progress*, the *Rake's Progress*, the *Marriage à la Mode* and the *Election* in which he ranges over every aspect of city life. Though his avowed purpose was to tell a story and point a moral—an end which has been dubiously regarded from his own time to ours—his art transcends this aim. Technically, also, Hogarth was a master of that delightful style of painting which belongs especially to his age, with its creamy lights and decision of touch. He had that force of genius that can animate a composition to the eye. His paintings, of abiding interest as an overall picture of 18th-century London life, are full of details that bespeak the artist and not the would-be moralist (Pl. 44).

The art of Thomas Rowlandson (1756–1827), although in the different medium of water-colour, companions that of Hogarth, though it was free from any pretensions to a literary or moralizing purpose. Rowlandson's social panorama, indeed, was even wider. He drew the places of fashionable entertainment and their visitors, as in his masterly picture of *Vauxhall Gardens*, as well as the crowded life of the mean streets (as in his *Rag Fair*), and in addition the life of rural England, the foxhunts, race meetings, fairs, the village alehouses, the shore and its nautical characters. With much coarseness and broad comedy of subject, Rowlandson is in no sense a vulgar artist. His restrained and delicate colour, and his gift for bringing a multitude of details together into a lively and unified composition, make his work a source of lasting delight.

In the 19th century the genre picture declined. An interest in trivial and anecdotal subjects together with a tendency to sentimentalize were now dominant at the expense of either truthful observation or of beauty of painting and drawing. David Wilkie, (1785–1841) shows ability in painting the simple humours of village life in the manner of the artists of the Netherlands as in his *Blind Man's Buff*, but his skill is somewhat empty of thought or purpose. In the Victorian age the idea of genre, i.e., of painting intimate scenes of everyday life, expanded in several ways, of dubious value. Sir Edwin Landseer applied it to the animal world, crediting domestic animals with human characteristics. Sir Laurence Alma-Tadema used it to give an entertaining character to pictures professing to depict the social life of ancient Greece and Rome. A curious residue of the historical genre was the kind of picture produced c. 1880–1890 (in France and Italy as well as Britain) showing cardinals in their red robes and cavaliers merrily playing cards or bent over chess boards. These are meaningless as works of art, though some specious flavour of "olden times" accounts for their popularity, which is not quite extinct.

The idea that art had a more serious mission than to tell silly little stories showed itself in the reaction of the young Pre-Raphaelites (c. 1848) against the trivial humours of early Victorian art. In France the whole nature and theory of Impressionism was against it, Impressionism being unconcerned with stories of any kind, and regarding life and nature as a spectacle of colour. In our own time there is a general decline of the subject picture and a reaction against anecdote or story. It seems hardly likely to revive as a study of "low life" in an age when life becomes more and more standardized and without social variety. One interesting survival in Britain is the work of Charles Spencelayh who paints old folk in old-fashioned interiors, depicting with loving care the fruit under glass domes, the Victorian engravings, the clutter of furniture of a past age. Yet this, as the subjects convey, is a survival, and our own hurrying period seems unamenable to record of this kind.

CHAPTER V

PORTRAITURE

SOME of the world's greatest pictures are portraits. Their greatness consists in something more than a photographic likeness. A photograph gives, mechanically, an impression, in which there are no definite outlines, and the main areas of light and shade do not necessarily correspond with the essential structure of the sitter's features. A master draughtsman like Holbein, however, even without the aid of colour or elaborate modelling, is able to select and concentrate the character of his subject into a decisive outline. Then again, a photograph can only give a view of a person at one particular moment. As human expression is the sum of a number of varying emotions, it follows that the camera portrait recorded in a split second may be quite untypical even though we can recognize the person portrayed. For the great artists the likeness is not something elusive and fleeting; it pervades, and actually is in essence, the form and structure before his eyes (see El Greco's *Cardinal Don Fernando*, Pl. 52). The intuition which enables him to grasp character and his understanding of form can hardly be separated. Thus the portrait painter— as Mr. Augustus John has explained, with reference to his own work (Pl. 43)—is by no means bound to approach his task like a psychologist, setting down a mental appreciation. On the contrary he may be entirely absorbed in the various planes, the hills and valleys of the facial landscape before him: yet as if by magic these forms understandingly observed will contain in result the essential humanity of the sitter.

The first painted portraits to claim our notice are those Greco-Roman panels carried out in encaustic of which the National Gallery in London has excellent examples (Pl. 8). These are from the cases of mummies discovered in Egypt, 1888, by Professor

Flinders Petrie, and range in date from A.D. 40 to 250. They are not interesting solely for historical reasons but for their vivid humanity, and the secret of this is to be found in the way the artists have concentrated on the main features—eyes, mouth and general shape of the head. The eyes especially in each case magnetically hold the attention. There is no attempt at natural lighting or at the illusion of reality at which some modern portrait painters aim, but the absence of these qualities seems to add a special force and lifelike character to the essentials so firmly grasped.

In the Middle Ages, when attention was so much fixed on religious subjects, there was little individual portraiture, though from the 14th century onwards the practice grew of including in the group compositions of altarpieces portraits of the donor and benefactor of the Church, and sometimes also a self-portrait by the artist. The separate individual portraits that finally emerged were, naturally enough, those of royalty and of people of rank and wealth. In Italy the portrait medallion seems to have suggested painting in profile: the profile also had the advantage of clearly indicating the shape of features. A beautiful example is the portrait of a lady by Alessio Baldovinetti (1425–1499) in the National Gallery (Pl. 42). In its contrast of blue and gold, and the decorative detail of dress and coiffure, it may be looked at with pleasure simply as an arrangement of form and colour, though the facial outline is very personal and interesting. Other famous profile portraits are those of the Duke of Urbino and his wife (Uffizi Gallery, Florence) by Piero della Francesca, set against a delightful landscape distance.

The wealth of Flanders in the 15th century produced a demand for portraits which painters satisfied in a style of great distinction. A great masterpiece of early Flemish art is the double, full-length portrait of Giovanni Arnolfini and Giovanna Cenami by Jan van Eyck (Pl. 40). Arnolfini, a wealthy Italian merchant, and his bride-to-be stand in an attitude that suggests the ceremony of betrothal. The painting is full of wonderful merits. No one previously had contrived to bring two figures, as here, away from the background and set them in a space that has the aspect of three-dimensional reality. In his treatment of perspective van Eyck shows an unobtrusive mastery far beyond that of the early Italian students of this science, and the pose of the two figures is related in a most natural and human way. Apart from this, we note the loving care that has so exquisitely defined every shape, and the marvellous detail executed with the incomparable smooth brilliance of van Eyck's technique—the convex mirror in the background is a masterpiece in itself.

Artists in the Italian Renaissance tried to give psychological truth to portraiture, not simply by stressing certain main physical features but by the subtlety of light and shade. In this respect Leonardo da Vinci stands out as unique. The mingled subtlety and power of his modelling is seen in the wonderful self-portrait drawn in sanguine in his old age (Royal Palace, Turin), awe-inspiring in its suggestion of immense intellectual force. The decision of line is combined with the mystery of shadow. The famous *Mona Lisa* (Louvre), whose smile has had so great a fascination for mankind, carries this mystery of shadow further in oil painting, the faintly smiling expression coming from the delicate gradations of modelling about the mouth. Another height of portraiture is reached by the Venetians. It is bound up with the exploitation of the richness, depth and variety of treatment which the oil medium allowed. This can be traced in the brilliance of Giovanni Bellini's *Doge Leonardo Loredan* (National Gallery), the grandeur of Titian's elderly self-portrait (Prado) and Tintoretto's portrait of *Vincenza Morosini* (National Gallery) in which with a limited range of colour, broken and varied in a seemingly almost casual fashion, the worn features of the sitter are miraculously stamped with character.

Turning north and westwards, we find with the growth of humanism and the advent of the Reformation in the early 16th century that portraiture becomes the principal occupation of the artist. Hans Holbein the younger (1497–1543) stands out in both painting and drawing. The drawings in the Royal Collection, Windsor, of members of the English Tudor Court astonish us by their completeness and life, though the chalk outline is reinforced by only a slight suggestion of colour. The figures in some of his painted portraits are laden with costly trappings (Henry VIII and his Court seemed to have looked on a portrait as a sort of inventory of jewellery and fine clothes) but Holbein himself had a superb sense of the effectiveness of simplicity. This is shown by his masterpiece, one of the world's truly great pictures, *Christina, Duchess of Milan*, to be seen in the National Gallery (Pl. 47).

In the achievements of the 17th century, we note equally the artists' great feeling for humanity and that full development of the oil technique in which it is conveyed. Holland gives us Rembrandt towering above all his contemporaries. The darkness in which his portraits are wrapped, from which only the face and hands emerge into light, gives an impressive isolation to the personality of the sitter. The loaded pigment of his sad self-portraits, worked over with much retouching, ceases to be paint and becomes a living substance (Pl. 41). In Spain there is Velazquez to immortalize the features of Spanish royalty (Pl. 46), yet also to paint a court buffoon or dwarf with equal sympathy and truth. It is his skill in combining a simply and grandly conceived silhouette with crisp touches of light and colour that makes the whole vivid and resplendent. We see this in his portrait of the elderly Philip IV (National Gallery) or in those beautiful contrasts of blue-grey and rose which enliven the portrait of an Infanta. The Flemish painter Rubens, again, in the portrait of his second wife's sister, Susanna Fourment, employs his amazing skill to give a delicate pearly effect of flesh as if seen in the open air. There are two things that strike us in the work of these great men. Their portraits are unfailingly interesting as pictures, irrespective of the character or status of the sitter. They are not concerned with flattering

89

or giving magnificence to the sitter but with an essential humanity.

The ceremonial portrait is in a different and, generally speaking, as a work of art, a lower category. Van Dyck (1599–1641), a pupil of Rubens, contrived with great taste and refinement to impart an air of dignity and good breeding to his portraits, but his style contains the seeds of an artificiality which becomes wearisome in the later artists of the Stuart period, Sir Peter Lely and Sir Godfrey Kneller. In France, the reign of Louis XIV saw a good deal of merely official and pompous portraiture.

A more natural and unassuming style marks English art in the 18th century. The "conversation piece", in which members of a family or a group of friends are seen in unstudied and informal attitudes in customary or typical surroundings is one aspect of this. As practised by a great artist like Hogarth, or by lesser but still very able artists like Arthur Devis (1711–1787) or Johann Zoffany (1733–1810), it gives us valuable glimpses of the social life of the period. A famous early picture by Thomas Gainsborough (1727–1788) of Robert Andrews and his wife is a sort of open air conversation piece showing them in evident enjoyment of their East Anglian estate (Pl. 35). Hogarth, in single portraiture, is seen at his best in a wonderful sketch executed with three or four colours of a laughing girl, a cockney shrimp-seller. Sir Joshua Reynolds, typically represented by his *Nelly O'Brien* (Pl. 1), also excelled in portraits of those connected with the arts—Mrs. Siddons, Dr. Johnson, Laurence Sterne, Oliver

Goldsmith. Both Reynolds and Gainsborough were perhaps at their best in their appreciation of childhood. Gainsborough's paintings of his daughters have in particular this tender feeling for immature charm. His art, generally speaking, is distinct in style from that of any of his contemporaries in its free and delicate brushwork—a series of touches which at a proper distance magically produced their effect (Pl. 45). British portraiture, however, already showed signs of that deference to status, class and convention, which is the main temptation of this form of art. Raeburn, Romney, Hoppner, Opie, Sir Thomas Lawrence, were all painters who worked in the fine 18th century tradition, though as creative artists they did not attain to the level of Hogarth, Reynolds or Gainsborough.

In portraiture, as in other forms of art, it is in the long run the outlook and style of the artist that counts for most. Dr. Péral, of whom the great Spanish artist Goya (1746–1828) made a famous portrait (now in the National Gallery, London), is not perhaps of great interest today as an individual. We are in no position to gauge the accuracy of the likeness, though we may feel the portrait is so living that it must have been an accurate representation. We are, however, conscious of a passionate quality of observation that gives its own energy to the sitter, and also of the fluid delicacy of Goya's paint, with its restless lights, its silver-greys modified by touches of warm colour. Again the portraits by Vincent van Gogh of anonymous individuals—a Zouave, an Arlesian woman, a postman, are all remarkable works because of the artist's personal vision.

Among the masterpieces of the 19th century we must certainly include James McNeill Whistler's portrait of his mother (Louvre), which the artist himself invited the observer to consider as "an Arrangement in Grey and Black", rather than a likeness (Pl. 48). The beauty of tone, the perfect balance of spacing as between the seated figure and the paintings in the background, are the important factors in its effect on the eye, and it is in its way perfect though we may feel that the greatest masters, Velazquez for instance, would have added more depth of humanity without detriment to the design. If Whistler's idea of portraiture is an extreme, it throws into relief the fact that a would-be photographic likeness without personality in style and outlook is another and less admirable extreme, and one which, as it aims at a photographic effect, would be better left to the camera.

CHAPTER VI

THE HUMAN FIGURE

IN pictorial art the study or representation of the nude figure scarcely dates back earlier than the Italian Renaissance, that is to say, than the 15th century. The ancient Greeks conceived their ideal of human physical proportion in terms of sculpture;

and after the classical period and throughout the Middle Ages there was an aversion from the nude as a sinful and pagan thing. Artists turned to the figure once more, partly with the revival of interest in the art of the classical world and partly through the Renaissance desire for a complete knowledge and command of form. In this respect the Italian artists were more scientific than the Greeks (so far as we know) had been. They studied anatomical structure and even dissected bodies. Leonardo da Vinci made a whole series of beautifully drawn anatomical diagrams. All Michelangelo's work shows a complete understanding of the construction of the figure. Many drawings of the nude survive from their period. Sometimes they were made simply for study, sometimes as a sketch for a figure in a painting. We often find that groups of figures, even if they were to appear clothed in a finished work, were first drawn in the nude. In this way essentials of structure and movement could be realized and retained, whatever subsequent draperies and details of costume were added.

The value of the human figure, from the artist's point of view, apart from the fact of its being human, lies in its variety and subtlety of rounded form and surface, greater than in any other form in nature. In repose or action it presents ever new and interesting relations of shape, problems which the artist delighted to solve. With the Renaissance artists it was also a means of asserting the importance of the human being. The shivering, naïvely drawn forms of those condemned to Hell in a religious picture of the Middle Ages were replaced by figures of magnificent physique. The stories of Greek gods and goddesses gave an excellent pretext for the idealization of male vigour or feminine beauty as shown in Raphael's *Three Graces* (Pl. 55); though a limited number of religious subjects also could be made the vehicle of the Renaissance artist's newly acquired anatomical science.

Thus the Florentine Antonio Pollaiuolo (1432–1498), one of the first specialized students of anatomy, aimed at the expression of vigorous muscular movement in both secular and religious themes. His *Hercules slaying the Hydra* (Florence, Uffizi Gallery) draws attention to the play of muscles as the hero raises his club. Again, in his *Martyrdom of S. Sebastian* (National Gallery) the main interest resides in the circle of muscular bowmen and the physical tensions produced as they bend to wind their cross-bows or lift them to shoot their arrows at the saint (Pl. 51). The representation of sheer muscular energy reaches its most superb point in the wall and ceiling paintings of the Sistine Chapel in the Vatican, by Michelangelo (1475–1564). Colossal limbs are modelled with a sculptor's sense of solid form, and exaggerated with a violence that speaks of Michelangelo's own temperament. A warning addressed to the "too-anatomical painter" to be found in the writings of Leonardo, seems to criticize this element in Michelangelo's art. Yet his reclining figure of Adam, to single this out from an immense array of figures, is in itself one of the supreme feats of genius in painting.

In contrast, another Florentine of genius, Sandro Botticelli (1445–1510), fascinates us with a delicate and graceful ideal of feminine beauty in his universally celebrated *Birth of Venus* (Uffizi). The beauty of line plays a great part in Botticelli's work and is well seen here in the slender silhouette of Venus, blown to the shore in her shell by the winds on either side (Pl. 29). The same linear beauty is to be found in the less celebrated but delightful *Mars and Venus* by Botticelli in the National Gallery. Venus has a typical gravity of expression while the sleeping figure of Mars is natural without forcibly impressing us with the artist's anatomical learning.

The beauty of the female figure was a main theme of the Venetian painters of the Renaissance and the more sensuous character of Venetian art seemed apter to convey it than the intellectual art of Florence. This sensuous character is also to be seen in the figure paintings of Correggio who worked mainly at Parma. The artists of Venice, better than any others perhaps, were able to combine in their figures a universally appealing physical attraction with a richness of form and colour that are magnificent in themselves. The short-lived Giorgione (1477–1510) was the pioneer of this sensuous art and two famous pictures, the *Concert Champêtre* (Louvre) and *The Storm* (Accademia, Venice), both entirely without narrative or story interest, bring a new and poetic element into figure painting (Pl. 54). Titian worked with Giorgione and was to some extent his pupil. Giorgione's pictures are static and contemplative. Titian, equally interested in rich physical substance, adds vigour and movement. One great picture by Titian is the so-called *Sacred and Profane Love* (Rome, Borghese Gallery) in which two women, one fully clothed and the other unclothed, seem to converse by the side of a sculptured well-head. The contrast is story enough and one can weave any fancy into it, but the beauty of the picture resides in the rounded perfection and graceful poise of a nude figure worthy of a Greek sculptor, seen against a mellow evening landscape. Mention has been made in an earlier chapter of the joyous movement of the figures in Titian's *Bacchus and Ariadne*. There are many more masterpieces of figure painting by him, including the *Bacchanal* (Prado, Madrid), *Venus and Adonis* (National Gallery) and the *Perseus and Andromeda* (Wallace Collection, London).

The figure painting of Titian was greatly admired and studied by masters in the 17th century. Nicolas Poussin (1594–1665) seeks to rival his *Bacchanal*, though Poussin lacks the Venetian warmth. Rubens (1577–1640) aims at a similar richness in composition and flesh painting, as in the *Judgement of Paris* (National Gallery). Velazquez (1599–1660) is inspired by Titian to paint a *Venus* (the so-called *Rokeby Venus* in the National Gallery), the only nude by this great realist (Pl. 49). It is interesting to see how Rubens and Velazquez, each in his own way, depart from the Italian mode of idealizing the figure. The nude of Rubens has a weightiness that belongs to his own character and country. The nude

33. PIETER DE HOOCH
Boy Bringing Pomegranates

34. PIETER BRUEGHEL: *The Village Wedding*

35. THOMAS GAINSBOROUGH: *Robert Andrews and his Wife*

Louis Le Nain
The Concert

36. Hans Holbein
Detail from *The Ambassadors*

37. JAN VERMEER
The Guitar Player

38. FRANCISCO DE GOYA
Majas at a Balcony

39.   EL GRECO
The Burial of Count Orgaz

40.   JAN VAN EYCK
*The Marriage of Giovanni Arnolfini and
Giovanna Cenami*

41. REMBRANDT
Self Portrait

42. ALESSIO BALDOVINETTI
Portrait of a Lady

43. AUGUSTUS JOHN
Portrait of Miss Eve Kirk

44. WILLIAM HOGARTH
The Times of Day—Morning

45. THOMAS GAINSBOROUGH
Mary, Countess Howe

46.   DIEGO VELAZQUEZ
Philip IV when Young

47. HANS HOLBEIN
Christina of Denmark, Duchess of Milan

48. JAMES MCNEILL
WHISTLER
The Artist's Mother

of Velazquez is a posed model: superbly painted as she is and in spite of the winged Cupid who holds up her looking-glass, she is clearly in the studio and not in some Arcadian country of the imagination.

If we turn to Rembrandt the break with idealism may be disturbing at first, for Rembrandt does not even choose attractive models but the homely creatures about him, whose imperfections he makes no attempt to disguise. Here we have the clearest distinction between the beauty of a painting and the different beauty of real life. A female nude by Rembrandt, squat and ugly as the figure may seem, is nevertheless a wonderful form when invested with the magic of his light and shade. In fact, as we study the subsequent history of the nude in art, we are struck by the many changes which are due to the purpose or character of the artist. The Spanish artist Goya gives us (like his compatriot Velazquez) one masterpiece, the *Maja Desnuda* of the Prado, and we are conscious not only of a realistic intention but of a certain sardonic sensuality in the painter. In 18th-century France we find a playful adaption of the old classic themes for the decoration of a royal palace or an aristocratic pavilion. François Boucher (1703–1770) was adept in this art, the frivolous and artificial character of which has been often criticized. Yet we must not be unduly prejudiced on this account any more than against Rembrandt because of his plain models. A masterly skill lay behind Boucher's artificial charm.

In various ways 19th-century artists sought to revive what they thought to be the classical spirit in depicting the human figure. Jacques Louis David (1748–1825), reacting both against the style of Boucher and the society to which he belonged, painted compositions which were a sort of propaganda for the republican virtues of Rome. He depicted its inhabitants, as in his *The Sabine Women* (Louvre), in a severe fashion and without the attraction of colour, like sculpture (Pl. 60). David had great influence throughout Europe, though his later years were spent in Brussels, after he had been exiled from France as a regicide. In terms of art he upheld the strict discipline of figure drawing and this was the main idea of his principal pupil, J. A. D. Ingres (1780–1867). How beautifully Ingres drew is perhaps best shown by his pencil portraits, small masterpieces of delicate precision. In his painting there is some conflict between the dry style he learnt from David and his own much less austere natural tendency. *La Source*, a simple study of a nude girl at a well, was long considered to be his masterpiece, though it gives a somewhat insipid ideal of beauty, the sentiment of which is critically viewed today.

Certainly the great figure paintings of the 19th century are those of French artists. Britain had a devoted student of the nude in William Etty (1787–1849) who painted flesh with some of the richness of Rubens and the Venetians, but his many admirable sketches of single figures in oil colours never led to the production of a masterpiece. A belated "classic" revival in the later 19th century, represented by the work of Lord Leighton, Sir Edward Poynter and Albert Moore, displays a somewhat cold and lifeless idealism. The best work of the century was that which was contemporary in its realism, and in this realism the French led the way. A magnificent picture is the "allegory of real life" painted by Gustave Courbet in 1855, *The Studio*, in which the artist depicts himself at his easel with a nude model and in the background various friends and contemporary types. Courbet is followed by Edouard Manet who with brilliant skill brought old master themes up to date. Thus his famous picture of a picnic party, the *Déjeuner sur l'Herbe* (Louvre), shows an unclothed model who has been bathing, sitting in a glade with fully dressed male companions. The picture caused a great scandal on that account, though Manet was using a theme long ago employed by Giorgione. In the same way his *Olympia* (Louvre) is a brilliant modern version of the reclining nude of Titian, though again the realistic treatment caused a storm of controversy. Manet was followed by two masters whose art was at its best in depicting the female figure, Auguste Renoir and Edgar Degas. Renoir beautifully renders in some works the play of colour and light on the figure; the paintings of his later years have a joyous warmth which exemplifies his remark that figures should be painted like so much lovely fruit. Degas, on the other hand, is interested in the unconventional poses and gestures of real life, as, for example, those of getting into or out of a bath, and in the swift medium of pastel

99

he makes a unique record of humanity caught unawares (Pl. 7).

While the works discussed above come under the heading of realism, it is clear that what makes them of value as works of art is some personal distinction in the artist's style or some originality of observation. Without either of these qualities realistic painting of the nude, in a photographic sense, can be the most boring form of art. On the whole, in this century, though one could mention a number of capable studies of the nude, it would seem as if the figure— at all events for the time being—has ceased to be a main theme of art, in its two principal abstract and imaginative forms. There are important exceptions to this generalization. The Italian painter Modigliani, for instance, while simplifying and distorting form in a modern way, shows something of his great fellow-countryman Botticelli's appreciation of the figure as a beautiful organism. Or again, there is Augustus John, whose splendid drawings of the female figure recall those of the Renaissance. Picasso, too, in his constantly variable work, has used the theme of nymph and faun in playfully simplified outline; while a remarkable series of drawings of artist and model in changing mood and aspect has great brilliance. It is in graphic art rather than in painting that the modern artist has produced the most distinguished figure work.

CHAPTER VII

ANIMALS IN ART

THE first masterpieces of animal drawing and painting are those of cave-men in prehistoric Europe. The caves are located in south-west France, the Dordogne, and north Spain. The types of human culture associated with them have been named after main sites; thus the Aurignacian culture (from Aurignac, S.W. France) is the earliest, and the Magdalenian (from La Madeleine, Dordogne) is the later form. Dates are somewhat speculative, but the first phase may have begun as early as c. 40,000 B.C., and the art of the caves stretches thereafter over a period of probably more than 20,000 years. In this immense period we must suppose that man flourished in the warmer intervals between ice-age conditions. He knew and depicted animals adapted to cold and only now surviving as fossils, the mammoth and woolly rhinoceros. Among the other animals he drew are the bison, wild boar, reindeer, stag, ibex, cave bear, wild horse and pony. His art has survived partly through being immured in caves only rediscovered in the 19th century and subsequently; partly because he used for pigment unchanging carbon black and red earth, which again have often received a natural permanent varnish from the drip of the cave that has hardened with time into a glaze. In the cave-man's world, animals were obviously the all-important factor and (as mentioned earlier) he drew them for a purpose, that is, to exercise some sort of magic power over them. This in itself, however, would scarcely prepare us for masterpieces such as were found in the Aurignacian cave of Lascaux or the Magdalenian cave of Altamira. It remains astonishing that these early folk were great artists. This is to be seen in the unerring instinct with which they selected precisely those forms and outlines which were most characteristic of the animal; adding a kind of shading which vividly conveys its bulk. The bison of Altamira (Pl. 10), or the wild horses of Lascaux, show a powerful simplicity which modern artists have not only admired but tried to imitate.

Between these and the admirable drawings and paintings of animals found in rock shelters or caves in southern Africa, it is impossible to establish any link of date or influence. All we can say is that the natives of Africa who produced the latter lived under much the same conditions as the Old Stone Age man, and show a similar perception and skill in depicting the animals they knew, types of deer for instance being drawn with delicate truth and a sense of grouping that the prehistoric cave-men lacked.

Artists of the Orient, in historic times, though belonging to highly developed civilizations, show a certain kinship of style with these primeval examples. Chinese and Japanese artists particularly display the gift of selection, bringing out the characteristic form of a bird or animal with a few decided strokes of the brush (Pl. 11). Their purpose of course was quite different from that of the cave-man. Animal drawing was not a form of magic but part of a philosophy that looked with sympathy on all created things, and very often one finds a touch of understanding humour. The manuscript paintings of Persia and India likewise contain beautifully observed horses, gazelles or elephants.

In comparison, animal painting or drawing in Europe during the Middle Ages is sadly crude. Animals sometimes suggested to the artist a fear— some grotesque forms, or otherwise were depicted with complete indifference to their real aspect or structure. The cloistered seclusion and prejudices of monkish artists may be partly responsible. It was not until the 15th century that the habit of careful observation prevailed. The art of Pisanello (c. 1390–1451), for instance, provides a series of detailed and faithful studies of animals from life. His painting in the National Gallery, the *Legend of St. Eustace*, indicates what good use he made of them. His beautiful study of a greyhound (Pl. 59) may be placed with Albrecht Dürer's famous drawings of animals (Pl. 58) among the classics of this branch of art. Animals and birds have from his time onward frequently appeared in the paintings of European artists, not as the main subject, but reflecting the wide range of their skill and their interest in every kind of life. These animal "extras" form an entertaining item in the anthologies of pictorial detail published by the National Gallery.

One is constantly struck by the understanding they show. Nothing could be more dog-like than the expression and silhouette of the hound, Laelaps, in *The Death of Procris* (Pl. 59) by the Florentine painter Piero di Cosimo (1462–1521), or in a different way the little griffon, its wiry hair so minutely painted, that stands at the feet of Giovanni Arnolfini and his fiancée in Jan van Eyck's masterpiece. The kitten that springs on the back of a chair in Hogarth's portrait group of the Graham children is sparkling with mischief. The lion that rolls over in Ruben's *Peace and War* is a magnificent study of relaxed ferocity.

Yet one notices in all these works that the animal plays some subsidiary part in pictures of which the main theme is human beings. This is probably as it should be, and rather adds to the interest than otherwise. In painting, animal portraiture tends to have a limited and specialized value. Thus *The Bull* by the Dutch artist Paul Potter (Hague, Mauritshuis) was long regarded as a masterpiece, though to modern eyes the bovine portrait does not seem to serve any important purpose. Paintings of racehorses are for the most part dull as works of art, however useful as a record to their owners and breeders. It may be that this is only another way of saying that a work of art must possess some definite quality of form, colour or feeling that comes from the artist and is distinct from careful imitation. Another picture by a 17th-century Dutch artist, Carel Fabritius, *The Goldfinch* (Hague, Mauritshuis) is no more than a simple study of a bird perched on its food trough, yet it is in its way a little masterpiece (Pl. 58). One may ask why it should merit this title when Potter's ably painted bull does not. The design for one thing has much more personality: that is, the relation of one form to another is much more carefully considered than in Potter's picture, and even the placing of the bird on the canvas adds to the profound sense of life it gives.

The British school of sporting art which flourished in the latter half of the 18th and the first half of the 19th centuries must be judged as art by the same standard, and a good deal of it, it must be confessed, is somewhat wooden and unimaginative. The racing scenes by John Wootton (c. 1688–1765), Peter Tillemans (1684–1734) and James Seymour (1702–1752) have the attraction of their period and the glamour of the national sport. Ben Marshall (1767–1835), J. F. Herring (1795–1865) and Henry Alken (active 1816–1831) are often spirited in their rendering of fox-hunting scenes and the other field sports. As artists, however, these men belong to a minor category. Only two painters much concerned with animals stand out—George Stubbs (1724–1806) and George Morland (1763–1804). Stubbs, with a thorough understanding of the horse's anatomy, gives it a certain grandeur of form achieved by none of his sporting contemporaries (Pl. 56). Morland was a natural painter who was able to combine with great charm landscape, figures, horses and farmyard animals into compositions representing typical country life. The British tradition of animal painting continued with his brother-in-law, James Ward (1769–1859), whose *Landscape with Cattle* (Tate Gallery) was an attempt to rival Paul Potter's *Bull*; and finally with Sir Edwin Landseer (1802–1873), famous in his day throughout Europe. In his capacity to draw animals Landseer may be compared with the follower of Rubens and painter of vigorous hunting scenes, Frans Snyders (1579–1657). He remains, however, one of the notable "test-cases" of art. Amusing a large public by attributing human sentiments to animals and representing them as typical Victorian characters, he certainly cheapened and falsified animal painting to a degree that made it worthless.

French artists of the 19th century offer a decided contrast in their appreciation of purely animal movement, vigour or ferocity. The horses of Baron Gros and Théodore Géricault are fiery steeds with something of the passionate movement which is to be found earlier in drawings of horses by Leonardo da Vinci and in Rubens' paintings of battle. Eugène Delacroix, like Rubens, was fascinated by the supple grace and ferocity of the lion and the tiger. It is this essential wildness that we find again in the drawings of the animal sculptor Antoine Louis Barye (1795–1875).

In modern times there has been a dwindling number of artists to draw and paint animals. This is no doubt partly due to the growing value of photography as a record of appearance and movement. It was not until the photographic experiments of Muybridge that the action of a galloping horse was demonstrated with accuracy and the old representation of the horse with both fore and hind legs outstretched was shown to be a manifest impossibility. For information as to bird and other wild life, the snapshot and the film often have many advantages. On the other hand, the endless varieties of structure in the animal world still have their appeal to the imaginative artist. Picasso's illustrations to the *Natural History* of Buffon or the modern British painter Graham Sutherland's use of the grasshopper as a pictorial motif are examples.

CHAPTER VIII

STILL LIFE

IN still life painting, artists represent objects of various kinds not because they have some special meaning, value or story to tell, but because they allow the close study of form, light and colour without the distraction of an elaborate subject. The quality of the result depends entirely on the treatment; and it is the form of art to which many painters turn from personal choice when no specific subject is demanded from them by some particular market or social need. Anything serves the artist, even the most commonplace things around him, and it is one of his admirable functions to show with how much beauty and interest these may be invested (Pl. 62). A plate of fruit, a rose in a glass, a loaf of bread and jug of wine—these are subjects enough to call out the painter's skill and vision. The subject may not only be simple, it may even be, from the lay point of view, "ugly"—yet a great painter will demonstrate a magic of his own which converts this fancied ugliness into a noble work of art. A famous instance is *The Flayed Ox* (Louvre) by Rembrandt. A carcase hung up in a butcher's shop one would think was an ugly enough theme in all conscience, yet the eye of Rembrandt compels us to look at it in fascinated wonder. It was, no doubt, in a similar spirit, that Sosos, a Greek painter of the 3rd century, depicted an *Unswept Floor* with the debris of a banquet—a work surviving in a mosaic copy in the Lateran Museum, Rome.

These two examples, however, call for some effort to disregard unpleasing associations. More usually still life has an unobtrusive but agreeable and friendly connexion with things we all like to see, such as flowers, fruit, and the equipment of the table. One of the wall-painters of Pompeii (1st century A.D.) surprises us with a study of peaches and a glass jug in which there is quite a modern feeling for their material substance.

With other types of realism, still life disappeared in the Middle Ages when artists were preoccupied with their religious themes. It reappears in the 15th century in the form of details in subject pictures. The early Flemish painters, for instance, devoted equal care to every item in their composition—thus the chandelier and mirror in van Eyck's *Arnolfini* are painted with no less precision than the figures.

Later, Holbein in his group, *The Ambassadors* (National Gallery), adds a number of minutely painted still life objects: globes, a lute, an open book, etc. Here, though Holbein evidently intended some reference to the tastes and interests of the gentlemen portrayed, he obviously took a delight in the geometric forms of the globe and the musical instrument (Pl. 36). This quite abstract value in the shape of musical instruments has inspired a number of artists from his day to that of the Cubists.

The Italian painter Caravaggio (1573–1610) is one of those who illustrate this value. He was also one of the first to devote a picture to still life alone. The realism of which he was a pioneer is notable throughout the 17th century. The Spanish painter Zurbaran, a contemporary of Velazquez, paints a few lemons and oranges on a table top yet somehow gives them all that force of expression that is to be found in his paintings of monks and devotees. He establishes a geometric relation between fruit and dishes which makes every part of the picture a space held in tension with the rest. The forms take on a grandeur of their own as he emphasizes the depth of shadow.

The Netherlands, however, and especially the Dutch Provinces, most cultivated still life as a distinct form of art. In the 17th century the Dutch were already great horticulturists, and in consequence flower pictures came into great demand. The Dutch painters worked with amazing minuteness, though probably from drawings rather than direct from nature, for we sometimes find in the same floral composition flowers that bloom at different seasons. Often they would introduce some other small feature that gave scope for their delicate skill— a snail for example, or a drop of water sparkling on a leaf. Notable painters in this style were Jan Davidsz van Heem (1606–1684), who was overwhelmed with orders, the woman painter Rachel Ruysch (c. 1664–1750) and Jan van Huysum (1682–1749), all excellent in craftsmanship (Pl. 53).

The Dutch pride in the decoration of the table and in its good things is seen in another type of picture, in which the play of light on porcelain and glass, the texture of a richly patterned cloth, the curling peel of a half-cut lemon, the pearly grey of oysters, the ochre and rusty red of crabs and lobsters are rendered with the greatest appreciation of the quality of different surfaces by such painters as Willem Claasz Heda (c. 1594–1678) and Willem Kalf (1622–1693).

A greater artist than these was the French artist Chardin (1699–1779), exceptional for his choice of subject in his country and time. He belonged not to the aristocracy but to the bourgeoisie, and painted their homely and unpretentious interiors and domestic accessories. Chardin—and in this respect he rises far above the level of the Dutch still life painters—was able to give a few simple objects an inexhaustible interest. One can explain this in part by the masterly craft with which he used oil paint— the colour seems to create a luminous atmosphere round the forms—but in the long run we must add an intangible element which can only be described as Chardin's own sense of the endless wonder of visible things.

France remained, in the 19th century, the country where still life painting was most assiduously and brilliantly practised. Realism was the watchword of the century, and still life as well as landscape was a means of studying the effect of light and colour in nature—one of the main forms which Realism took. Claude Monet, leader of the Impressionists, gives us a kind of open air still life in his paintings of his garden at Giverny, his subject being growing flowers seen in sunlight and shown, in the Impressionist fashion, as so many patches of colour without outlines, presenting a luminous vibration to the eye. In the same spirit his fellow Impressionist, Alfred Sisley, painted the lilac trees in his garden at Moret. Courbet, Manet and Renoir, though we think of them mainly as figure and landscape painters, all painted brilliant studies of flowers or fruit. The art of still life comes into the forefront with the advent of Paul Cézanne and Vincent van Gogh.

Painting to Cézanne was a kind of research to be pursued without haste but with intense concentration. A dish of apples and a few simple table properties were sufficient to engross him deeply in the special task of translating the solidity of form into colour (Pl. 3). Each variation of surface, turned to or from the light, had its own special hue, and it can be appreciated how much effort the task of rendering it could absorb. For Cézanne, it was greatly in favour of still life that his models kept still. The self-imposed difficulty of his method did not in itself guarantee that the result would be a great work of art, yet Cézanne has the same profound interest as Chardin. He succeeds in giving grandeur to the fold of a table napkin, and his colour, fresh and delicate, is also a necessary part of the construction of his picture.

The Dutch painter van Gogh was not disciplined by Cézanne's purely aesthetic aim. He had an unrestrained delight in colour. He also transferred a dramatic quality to some of the objects he painted which gives them a special personal interest as symbols of his thought. His *Sunflowers*, now so popular for its radiant colour, is also a remarkable work for its passionate testimony to his worship of nature, his desire to put his whole being into his art (Pl. 63). These two painters, so different temperamentally each from the other, both demonstrate that still life is no bypath of art, nor a purely imitative exercise, but that it can be as lofty a means of expression as any.

CHAPTER IX

TRENDS IN MODERN ART

WHEN we look at the work of Claude Monet or Paul Cézanne we can see that in the later 19th century colour conveying some atmospheric mood of nature, or colour expressing form, was a factor of growing importance, and that the interest of objects or figures depicted was only secondary. Thus when Monet paints the porch of Rouen Cathedral he is little concerned with Gothic architecture, but gives us instead a sort of colour poem. Cézanne is not more interested in a human sitter than in a plate of apples, as for him in either case the problems of form and colour are the same. This tendency to abstract or separate the main visual constituents of a work of art from the documentary interest or value of recorded fact has grown in various ways, until finally we have a kind of painting that does not attempt representation at all and is sometimes called "non-figurative" or "abstract".

This kind of art has various degrees. All the great works of the past have an abstract element, though they may contain much besides. Nor, on the whole, does the art of the 20th century lack the figurative element. Yet broadly speaking there has been a change of emphasis. The artist's means of expression have been used in a freer and more venturesome fashion than before. There has also been a tendency to value "expression" in itself more highly than imitative skill.

Thus the earliest of the striking 20th-century movements, known as Fauvism, was an attempt to use colours for their own emotional value, and not merely because they described something such as a red dress or a blue skirt. It is best studied in the work of the French painter Henri Matisse, who aims at that kind of harmony that Oriental artists have achieved between areas of flat pure colours chosen for their decorative brilliance in relation to one another. Matisse remained a "figurative" artist, though his figures were carefully simplified in conformity with the general simplification of his style (Pl. 57). One of his followers was André Derain who in 1907 painted a picture of the *Pool of London* which is an excellent example of the Fauve method. The yellow green of the water, the bright reds and blues of ship and barges are such perhaps as were never seen on the Thames, yet the brilliant key is maintained so consistently and well that the picture gains its own truth. The living British painter Sir Matthew Smith, who studied for a while with Matisse, has also shown the value of an intensified pitch of colour.

The study of form in itself, as distinct from colour, led to the development of Cubism around 1907. Cézanne had stressed the underlying geometry of forms in nature, and it was this geometric principle that gave the impetus to this immensely influential movement. Searching for basic structure, the Cubists were led to sacrifice external appearance and to analyse and dissect forms on canvas, even to the extent of showing various viewpoints of an object in the same picture. A characteristic product was the Cubist still life. Here one might see familiar objects, a café table, coffee cup, glass, pipe, newspaper and so on, but reconstructed into a new kind of picture pattern.

To appreciate the results of the movement one must study the work of its two leaders, Pablo Picasso and Georges Braque. The development of

Picasso is full of interest and shows great accomplishment before he entered on his Cubist phase. His many studies of jugglers, acrobats and circus types, of which an example is given (Pl. 61), form an attractive facet of his many-sided art. Yet this was left behind in the enthusiasm for geometric construction which led both him and Braque into the adventure of Cubism, c. 1907. The early Cubist pictures of both, carried out in grey and ivory tones, and creating a sort of intricate scaffolding of planes and angles, have an austere impressiveness. In later works (after the 1914–1918 war) there is more colour, and the forms are flat and linear. The decorative character of Cubism came into prominence. Braque shows very strongly this sense of pattern and texture in many variations on the familiar theme of table top, bowl of fruit and mandoline (Pl. 64). Picasso, in some works, gives an almost heraldic value to Cubism in the counterchange of colours in well defined areas.

As a source of design or ideas of design Cubism had a great influence. It helped to encourage a constructive approach to the problems of modern architecture and the design of industrially produced goods. It had a limited though salutary influence on the design of posters. Its influence has appeared in designs for the stage and ballet. In fact, in general the modern artist has shown an adaptability to design in which he has gained from being no longer confined to realistic representation. A present-day tendency to entirely "non-figurative" painting has, however, another source than geometrical Cubism.

It can be traced to the idea that painting should be the fruit of intuition, entirely divorced from external reality. It was observed that children produced remarkable paintings and drawings up to the age of adolescence by some natural gift. Can the adult artist retain or make use of a similar unconscious source? This is the thought behind the abstract or non-figurative art of today, which has its practitioners in Britain, France, Germany and the United States. The value of the results is very much a matter of opinion, but like other forms of art it is not to be condemned unseen or by general statements. Each form of expression requires appraising individually. New ideas have been necessary at all times to stimulate artists, yet we must not confuse the matter by assuming that art progresses and gets better and better from age to age. The most novel form of art must eventually be judged in relation to the eternal verities of form and colour.

PART FIVE

Glossary of Terms in Common Use

ACADEMIC. Often used to suggest conventional accuracy in a work of art apart from original or expressive character.

ACADEMY. Denotes both a school of art and a society of artists. The first Academy of art was the Guild of St. Luke, founded in Venice in 1345. A French Royal Academy was founded in 1648 and the English Royal Academy in 1768.

ALLA PRIMA. Method of direct painting without retouching: cf. French *Premier Coup*.

ALTARPIECE. An altar decoration, consisting of a painted panel or panels, often with an elaborate carved or sculptured frame. The form taken by many great works of religious art from the Gothic period onwards.

BALANCE. In a painting, the equilibrium between forms or areas of light and shade of unequal extent.

BAROQUE. Term describing some general characteristics of European art in the 16th and 17th centuries. (See p. 46.)

BISTRE. Brown tint made from wood soot, often used in old master drawings.

BITUMEN. Medium made from pitch, formerly used to add richness to oil paintings, but prone to crack and darken disastrously as some pictures by Reynolds show.

BLACK. The total absence of light, sometimes loosely referred to as a colour. Carbon black pigments which are unchanging have been used by artists since the earliest times.

BYZANTINE. Post-classical art, centred in Constantinople and surviving in the Eastern Mediterranean lands until the 15th century. (See p. 42.)

CABINET PICTURE. Small picture, not intended to occupy one fixed and permanent position.

CAMERA OBSCURA. Apparatus for throwing an actual reflected image on to the surface on which the artist works. Canaletto in his views of Venice is supposed to have used such a device.

CAPRICCIO OR CAPRICE. Usually an imaginary or fantastic combination of architectural and other elements in a picture.

CARTOON. Originally the large scale design traced by the fresco painter on a wall surface. Also used of any preparatory work, e.g. the cartoons of Raphael, paintings in distemper used as a guide by tapestry weavers. Application of the word to political or other drawings in periodicals dates from the 19th century.

CHIAROSCURO. The arrangement of light and shade in a picture, and also its gradation to convey a three-dimensional effect.

CHINESE WHITE. A white pigment from zinc oxide, used in water-colour painting to give an opaque effect.

CINQUECENTO. Literally "five hundred", term applied to Italian art of the period 1500–1600. Similarly, *Quattrocento* implies Italian art in the 15th century and *Seicento* in the 17th century.

CLASSICAL. Term applied to the great period of Greek art (5th century B.C.), and by association to works of comparable perfection, e.g. those of Raphael.

CLASSICISM. Attempted revival of the classical past. (See p. 51.)

COMPLEMENTARY COLOURS. As, theoretically, the three primary colours red, blue and yellow produce white, any one combined with a mixture of the other two produces this effect. Thus red is the complementary of green (the mixture of blue and yellow) and blue of orange (red and yellow).

COMPOSITION. The art of weaving together the various visual elements in a picture to give a well-balanced and coherent effect. Also the result of this process. It may be divided into Linear Composition, the arrangement of lines and silhouettes without the illusion of depth, Spatial Composition, concerned with the illusion of depth, and Colour Composition; but all may be combined together in unity in the same work.

DECORATIVE. Term applied to paintings designed to fit a particular space, or to harmonize suitably with a particular scheme of interior decoration and the style of other subjects. The term is sometimes loosely applied to any markedly stylized form of composition.

DESIGN. In traditional usage, the preliminary drawing for a picture, but more generally the plan or main conception and the extent to which this is evident in the finished work.

DISTEMPER. Paint prepared with water and size; sometimes used for large-scale decorative painting.

EASEL PAINTING. A picture of comparatively small size such as may be painted at an easel; not destined for a fixed position.

ETCHING. Process of graphic reproduction by which lines drawn through a wax surface on a metal plate are bitten into by acid, printed impressions then being taken. The process allows the artist all the freedom of drawing with a pen.

EXPRESSION. Not only the expression of features, etc., as depicted by an artist, but also the extent to which the artist has conveyed his own inner feelings or character.

FORESHORTENING. An effect of perspective and viewpoint by which the shape and proportion of figures are altered and made smaller to the eye, e.g. a prone figure or an arm extended towards the spectator.

FRESCO. Wall painting executed piece by piece on a fresh lime coating, the paint thus being incorporated with the mural surface. (See p. 30.)

GENRE. Painting of ordinary life, often with an element of humour or anecdote. (See p. 79.)

GESSO. Prepared surface of plaster as a ground for painting, used especially for tempera painting.

GLAZING. In oil painting, the application of a transparent colour thinly over an area of solid pigment. This solid pigment is always lighter in tone than the glaze, the effect thus being luminous and rich. Titian is noted for his use of the method.

GOTHIC. In painting, an art of detail and bright colour, as in the illuminated missals and altarpieces of northern and western Europe from the 13th to the 15th centuries. (See p. 44.)

GOUACHE. Water-colour painting in which opaque pigments diluted with water and gum are used.

GRISAILLE. Monochrome painting, historically sometimes used to give the effect of a sculptured relief.

GROUND. The prepared surface of the canvas or panel on which the painter works. In etching, the wax layer covering a metal plate, through which the artist draws with a needle.

HATCHING. Lines parallel or crossed, by which the artist suggests tone or shadow in a drawing or engraving. It is also used to add finish and modelling in tempera painting where no general repainting is possible.

HIGH LIGHT. The point or points of greatest brilliance in a picture, found on surfaces which reflect and do not absorb light. In oil painting, it is often rendered by an especially heavy touch of light pigment, which in itself catches the light, and in watercolour by leaving the surface of the paper untouched.

HORIZON. The line at which earth and sky appear to meet, in perspective situated at the height of the observer's eye.

HUE. Strictly, the colour obtained by mixing a primary and secondary colour, but often loosely describing any shade of colour.

ILLUMINATION. Painting accompanying manuscripts on vellum or parchment, the effect of which is heightened by the use of precious metal, e.g. gold.

ILLUSTRATION. Term applied to drawings mechanically reproduced, or engravings, decorating a book or bearing on its theme. It is also applied more generally and sometimes unfavourably to pictorial works which depend on a story or associated subject interest rather than entirely on their intrinsic merits of form and colour.

IMPASTO. In oil painting, the use of thick colour to give effects of solidity and strength. It is used more particularly in the light areas of a picture rather than in the shadows.

IMPRESSIONISM. Technically the replacement of outline and chiaroscuro by pure colour designed to give the natural effect of light. (See p. 52.)

INDIAN INK. Also known as Chinese Ink, the Chinese having been especially noted for its manufacture. A dense and indelible preparation from lamp-black.

KIT-CAT. A special size of canvas for portraits of something less than three-quarter length, like the portraits of members of the Kit-cat Club by Kneller (National Portrait Gallery, London).

LAKE. Type of pigment prepared from vegetable or animal substances, e.g. Crimson Lake.

LAY FIGURE. Jointed figure of human being or animal (especially horses), giving general anatomical structure and proportion and relation of limbs in various attitudes. Used mainly for painting draperies or studying a given pose in the absence of a living model.

LITHOGRAPHY. Form of graphic reproduction, in which prints are taken from a drawing made with greasy chalk or ink on stone or a prepared zinc plate. Both black-and-white and colour lithography have been consistently popular with artists from the early 19th century.

LITTLE MASTERS. Term applied to a number of 16th century engravers, followers of Durer, who worked on a very small scale. Thus it does not in the strict sense refer to artists of limited powers, though now often so used.

LOCAL COLOUR. The colour which belongs to a particular object, e.g. a red dress. The term is applied in a more general sense to setting, dress and accessories typical of some particular place or country, e.g. in an exotic scene.

LOUVRE. The great art gallery of Paris, formerly the royal palace, and containing the collections of the French monarchs from the time of Francis I, and many late additions. It combines for France the functions of the London National Gallery and the British Museum, being rich both in antiques and pictures.

MANNERISM. Referring in a general sense to tricks of style, this word has a more specific reference to Italian art in the period (16th century) when the great works of the Renaissance inspired many imitations and exaggerations of their style.

MASTERPIECE. Historically, the work by which a young artist proved his skill in craftsmanship and was admitted as "master". Now applied either to the main work of any individual artist or to works of undisputed greatness in character and execution.

MAULSTICK OR MAHLSTICK. Long stick of wood tipped with a pad of cloth or leather. Held by the painter in one hand and resting against his canvas it acts as a support for his wrist when putting in fine detail.

MEDIUM. The liquid vehicle with which pigments are mixed for use., e.g. oil or water.

MODELLING. Used primarily in regard to sculpture. Modelling in painting or drawing means the indication of planes in such a way as to give the effect of a rounded or three-dimensional figure.

NATURALISM. The use of contemporary subject matter in art as distinct from ideal, imaginary or historical subjects.

NOCTURNE. A term borrowed from music and used by Whistler to describe his pictures of evening effect, not simply as night-pieces but with a suggestion of music in arrangement and colour.

OCHRE. Earths coloured by oxide of iron, providing permanent pigments varying from yellow to orange red.

OLD MASTERS. Term applied to the great painters of the past in Europe, more especially to those of the Renaissance period.

OUTLINE. The essential element of drawing, the definition of an object by a line round it. It belongs purely to art as there are no outlines in nature.

PALETTE. The square or oval-shaped tray on which the artist lays out his colours, with a hole for holding by the thumb. Artists usually arrange colours on the palette in an established order, e.g. from warm to cool. The word is used in a wider sense to indicate the characteristic colour scheme of any particular artist.

PALETTE KNIFE. Flexible metal knife, used to mix colours on the palette. Sometimes, however, it has replaced the brush as a means of applying paint to canvas.

PANEL PICTURE. Picture painted not on canvas but on a wooden panel.

PASTEL. Process of painting or drawing with dry colour. (See p. 27.)

PASTICHE. A work deliberately imitating the style of some past master or school.

PERSPECTIVE. The science of representing objects at varying distances from the eye, one of its main principles being that receding parallel lines converge to a point on the horizon. It first became an important factor in art when studied by Italian painters of the 15th century, though it has often been disregarded without detriment to aesthetic effect. Aerial perspective is a term used in reference to the gradations of tone and colour which suggest distance, and has no mathematical basis like the linear perspective referred to above.

PICTURESQUE. In the most general sense, a subject worthy of being made into a picture, but the word is now linked with the love of quaint or irregular forms that grew up in the Romantic period, late 18th to early 19th centuries.

PINACOTHECA. Name given to the picture gallery in the Propylaea in the Acropolis of ancient Athens. The Romans used the term for the galleries of private collectors. It has been reapplied in modern times to public picture galleries, a famous example being the Old Pinakothek of Munich.

PLANES. A series of flat vertical surfaces parallel to the surface of a canvas, seen in perspective and establishing relations of size and distance between objects depicted and the eye of the spectator. The word also refers to the various flat surfaces set at an angle to one another of which any solid or rounded object is made up. A close study of these planes can be seen in the work of Cézanne.

PLASTIC. Primarily referring to the art of modelling in clay, wax, etc. "Plastic" is sometimes used of painting to describe the artist's sense of three-dimensional form and his ability to convey it on a flat surface.

PLEIN-AIR. Painting out of doors as practised by the French Impressionists. It leads the painter to the study of generally diffused light, and its effect on objects as distinct from the more clearly marked contrasts of light and shade produced by the lighting of a studio.

POINTILLISM. System of painting with dots of red, yellow and blue, practised by the 19th century French painters Seurat and Signac. It is also known as Divisionism and is akin in principle to the mechanical three-colour process of colour reproduction. (See p. 53.)

POLYPTYCH. Term used of altarpieces comprising a number of panels capable of being folded one over the other, thus exposing different paintings to view.

PRADO. The national gallery of Spain, at Madrid, noted for its collections of paintings by Italian Renaissance and Flemish masters, reflecting the tastes of Charles V and Philip II, and also for its unrivalled collection of works by Velazquez, Goya and other Spanish masters.

PRE-RAPHAELITISM. An attempt to bring greater sincerity into art, based partly on truth to nature and partly on the ideals represented by Italian art before the Renaissance. (See p. 52.)

PRIMARY COLOURS. The colours which cannot be compounded from any others: red, yellow and blue. The combination of any two is called a Secondary Colour. Set side by side in varying quantities, the primaries will give any shade or gradation of colour required.

PRIMING. The prepared ground on canvas or panel on which painters work.

REALISM. The aim of truthfully representing form and colour in existing objects without artificiality or convention of style. (See p. 52.)

RENAISSANCE. The great development of art, in the 15th and 16th centuries, which centred in Italy. (See p. 45.)

RESTORATION. As regards pictures this term mainly refers to oil paintings, and consists in the removal of discoloured varnish or additions not from the painter's own hand.

ROCOCO. Term applied to the ornate style of interior decoration and furnishing, in the 18th century, mainly exemplified by France, and to the light and artificial style of painting that aptly accompanied it, typified by Boucher. (See p. 47.)

ROMANESQUE. In pictorial art the severe and simple religious painting contemporary with Romanesque architecture (11th–12th centuries). (See p. 44.)

ROMANTICISM. Form of art largely distinguished by its subject matter, violent, poetic and emotional. (See p. 52.)

SALON. Yearly exhibition in Paris of the work of living artists, dating back to the 18th century when a *Salon des Arts* was held in the *Salon Carrée* of the Louvre.

SANGUINE. Red chalk, or drawing made with red chalk, a favoured medium with many old masters.

SCHOOL. Originally referring to the painter-pupils working in the studio of one master, the word is used more generally of any kindred group of artists,

49. DIEGO VELAZQUEZ: *The Toilet of Venus*

50.   LEONARDO DA VINCI
The Madonna of the Rocks

51. ANTONIO POLLAIUOLO
The Martyrdom of S. Sebastian

52. EL GRECO
Cardinal Don Fernando

53. JAN VAN HUYSUM
Flowers in a Vase

54. GIORGIONE
The Storm

55. RAPHAEL
The Three Graces

56. GEORGE STUBBS
*Sir Solomon and
J. Singleton*

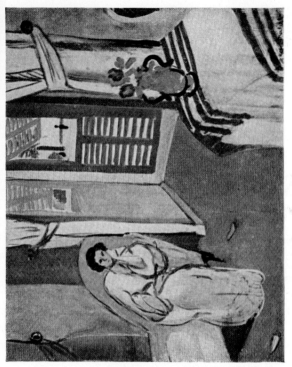

57. HENRI MATISSE
Figure in an Interior

Vienna

ALBRECHT DÜRER
Drawing of Squirrels

Mauritshuis, The Hague

58. CAREL FABRITIUS
The Goldfinch

PISANELLO: *Drawing of a Greyhound*

59.   PIERO DI COSIMO
Detail from *The Death of Procris*

60. J. L. DAVID: *The Sabine Women*

61 PABLO PICASSO
The Harlequin Family

PAUL SIGNAC: *The Water-melon*

62. H. FANTIN-LATOUR
Still Life

63. VINCENT VAN GOGH
Sunflowers

64. GEORGES BRAQUE: *Still Life*

usually in terms of locality or nationality, e.g. 'Norwich School', 'School of Paris', 'Dutch School'.

SCUMBLING. The modification of colour in a picture by dragging paint over it with a dry brush.

SEPIA. Warm brown tint, originally prepared from the ink of the cuttlefish, used in wash drawings.

SGRAFFITO (GRAFFITO). Italian method of scratching through a light superficial coating to a darker ground of paint or stucco, giving the effect of a drawing.

SILHOUETTE. Term applied particularly to small portraits which are either solid black on a white ground or solid white on a black ground. The same idea, more subtly treated and applying not necessarily to a head but to any area of a composition is used to great advantage by Velazquez and Whistler.

SPECTRUM COLOURS. The constituent colours of light which may be obtained by the refraction of a ray of light through a prism. As in the rainbow, there are seven: violet, indigo, blue, green, yellow, orange and red. The scientific fact helps us to understand the Impressionists' efforts to translate light into colour.

STILL LIFE. Painting of an inanimate object: cf. Fr. *Nature Morte*—"dead nature". (See p. 107.)

SYMBOLISM. The representation of a material object, not simply for its own interest or beauty, but as standing for an abstract idea. Thus virtues and vices have been symbolized in art in various human and animal forms. Religious art especially has made great use of symbols, e.g. the lamb, the dove.

TECHNIQUE. The artist's skill as a craftsman, his knowledge and mastery of materials and methods.

TEMPERA. Opaque painting with an egg medium.

TONE. In painting, the variations of a colour or of intermediate gradations between black and white, produced either by dilution or some by admixture with white. Thus a picture may be executed in light or dark tones. The term also refers to the dominant effect of colour, e.g. warm or cool.

TROMPE L'OEIL. A painting which deceives the eye in giving the impression of actually being what it represents. Thus painters have depicted what seems to the spectator to be a real fly on a canvas, or a torn piece of paper that seems to project from it. A kind of trick painting definitely to be distinguished from Realism.

VARNISH. A resinous preparation, passed over an oil painting when dry as a protection and preservative. It yellows and cracks with time and much care is then needed in its removal.

VEHICLE. The liquid with which pigments are diluted and applied to canvas or paper: oil, water or special emulsion according to the medium employed.

WASH. A flat tint of water-colour, sepia, etc., applied with a full brush to flow evenly over the paper.

WATER-COLOUR. Form of painting on paper with transparent colours. (See p. 27.)

PART SIX

Painters and Draughtsmen

BIOGRAPHICAL NOTES

Angelico, Fra (Fra Giovanni da Fiesole) (1387–1455). Trained as a Dominican friar, he is famous as a religious painter of the Florentine school, his frescoes, e.g. in the Convent of S. Mark, Florence, showing beauty of colour and a devout spirit.

Apelles (4th century B.C.). The most famous painter of ancient Greece who painted Alexander the Great and also subject pictures. He is said to have used only four colours, red, yellow, white and black. No works by him are known to exist.

Bellini. Artist family of Venice. **Jacopo Bellini** (c. 1400–c. 1470) is known mainly as a draughtsman and student of perspective. His sons were the painters, **Gentile** (1421–1507) and **Giovanni** (c. 1430–1516). The latter is outstanding as developing the art of oil painting in Italy. His work includes religious pictures and his portrait of Doge Loredan (National Gallery) is a well-known masterpiece.

Blake, William (1757–1827). Poet and painter, born in London. Produced coloured drawings and engravings remarkable for their imaginative power and beauty of design. His best works are his engravings to the *Book of Job* and his water-colours for Dante's *Divine Comedy*, 1827. A splendid collection of his work is in the Tate Gallery, London.

Bonnard, Pierre (1867–1947). French painter, noted for pictures of Paris and interiors with figures, in which there are vivid colour harmonies. He also executed decorative panels on a large scale, and delightful colour prints.

Bosch, Hieronymus (c. 1450–1516). Painter of the Flemish school, whose paintings of religious subjects or parables show an extraordinary imagination. A work satirizing human desires, the *Haywain*, and the so-called *Garden of Terrestrial Delights* (Prado, Madrid), full of strange symbolism, are among his masterpieces.

Botticelli, Sandro (c. 1444–1510). One of the great Renaissance artists of Florence. He worked for the Medici family, producing those pictorial fables and allegories which delighted the secular patron. His *Primavera*, personifying the seasons, c. 1478 (Uffizi, Florence) and *Birth of Venus*, c. 1485 (Uffizi) are among the world's most beautiful compositions. Influenced by the doctrines of Savonarola he later returned to religious art, and his *Pietà* (Pinakothek, Munich) and *Nativity* (National Gallery, London) show deep feeling.

Braque, Georges (1882–). French painter, noted as the originator of Cubism (together with Pablo Picasso). Characteristic paintings by him are of still life in which familiar objects are freely reconstructed and arranged without regard to normal appearances but in decorative relation to one another.

Brueghel. Flemish artist family, of which the greatest member was **Pieter Brueghel the Elder** (c. 1520–1569). He is famous for superb pictures of peasant life. His masterpieces, *Children's Games; Hunters in Snow, February; Peasant Dance* and *Village Wedding* are at Vienna. Of his two sons, **Pieter** (known as "Hell") **Brueghel** (c. 1564–1637) and **Jan** ("Velvet") **Brueghel** (1568–1625), the latter was more distinguished and originated the flower picture in the Netherlands.

Canaletto, Giovanni Antonio (1697–1768). Venetian painter famous for his views of Venice. A favourite with English collectors, he is well represented in the National Gallery. He spent some years in England producing admirable pictures of Westminster and the Thames.

Caravaggio (Michelangelo Amerighi, 1573–1610). Italian painter, studied in Milan and made a great reputation in Rome by his powerful realism and effects of light and shade. In a wandering and sombre career he painted also fine works at Naples, Malta and Messina. His art was studied and imitated widely in Europe.

Carpaccio, Vittore (c. 1450–1525). Venetian painter, pupil of Gentile Bellini. He represents the life of his time in ostensibly religious pictures with a wealth of detail.

Carracci. Italian artist family, of which the principal member was **Annibale Carracci** (1560–

1609). His brother, **Agostino** (1557–1602) worked with him in Bologna and other cities. Their cousin **Lodovico Carracci** (1555–1619) founded a famous school at Bologna. Scholarly artists, they tried to combine the various excellences of the great Renaissance masters in their work.

Cézanne, Paul (1839–1906). French painter, born at Aix-en-Provence where he at last retired to work after study in Paris. In his study of the essentials of form he had immense influence on modern art. He excelled in landscape and still life. A famous picture is his *Mont Ste Victoire* (National Gallery).

Chardin, Jean Baptiste Simeon (1699–1779). French painter, born in Paris, greatly esteemed for his paintings of still life and bourgeois interiors with figures. His best works are in Paris in the Louvre.

Chirico, Giorgio di (1888–). Italian painter, born in Greece, noted for imaginative works in which there is a surrealist element.

Cimabue (1240–1302). Florentine painter whose work marks the end of Byzantine convention and the beginning of a great development in Italian art, as shown in frescoes by him at Assisi and a famous *Madonna with Angels* (Louvre).

Claude (Claude Gellée, otherwise known as Claude Lorraine, 1600–1682). French landscape painter who worked mainly in Rome. His "classical" landscapes combine beautiful renderings of dawn and sunset with fanciful architecture and subjects. The National

Gallery contains famous masterpieces by him. He made superb drawings of the country round Rome.

Constable, John (1776–1837). English landscape painter, born at East Bergholt, who brought the freshness of nature into paintings of typically English country, using broken colour with great skill to convey atmospheric effect. He had a strong influence on the development of French landscape in the 19th century. His work can be studied at both the National Gallery and the Victoria and Albert Museum, London.

Corot, Jean Baptiste Camille (1796–1875). French painter famous for landscapes with a poetic and silvery quality. He worked in Italy and in France, more especially at Barbizon. His figure studies arc also now much esteemed.

Correggio (Antonio Allegri, 1489–1534). Italian painter who worked mainly at Parma. He is noted for figure paintings in which there is a melting softness of shadow, a typical masterpiece being his *Mercury, Cupid and Venus* (National Gallery).

Cosimo, Piero di (c. 1462–1521). Florentine painter of mythological subjects in which he shows a delicate linear quality of design and a quaint fancy. A famous picture (National Gallery) shows a satyr grieving for a nymph.

Cotman, John Sell (1782–1842). British landscape painter, born at Norwich. He is noted for a style of water-colour which gives great value to silhouette. A masterpiece in this art is his *Greta Bridge, Yorkshire* (British Museum).

Courbet, Gustave (1819–1877). French painter whose aim was to represent only "real and existing objects" (Realism). His picture of a peasant funeral, the *Burial at Ornans* (Louvre), shows one aspect of this aim. He also painted powerful landscapes and still life.

Cozens. Father and son. **Alexander Cozens** (c. 1700–1786) invented a system of evolving landscape compositions from more or less accidental blots. His son, **John Robert** (1752–1799), was a water-colourist important in the history of British landscape for his views of Alpine scenery.

Cranach, Lucas (1472–1553). German painter and engraver, mainly distinguished by the naïve charm of his paintings of the nude figure, with some allegorical titles. Of these he executed many, e.g. *Venus* (Louvre), *Jealousy* (National Gallery).

Crome, John (1768–1821). Founder of the "Norwich School" and one of the great British landscape painters. Famous pictures by him are: *Slate Quarries* (Tate Gallery) and *The Poringland Oak, Moon Rise on the Yare* and *Mousehold Heath* (National Gallery). He also painted some excellent water-colours.

Daumier, Honoré (1808–1879). French painter and lithographer. Caricature, political and social, occupied much of his life. Apart, however, from his satirical pictures of French middle-class society in *Le Charivari* he produced about a hundred paintings, Rembrandtesque in light and shade but highly individual.

David, Jacques Louis (1748–1825). French painter who represents the desire to return to the antique. Among his pictures of antique themes, somewhat cold and formal in style, his *Sabine Women* (Louvre) is typical. His *Death of Marat* is an impressive work and he excelled in portraiture, his *Mme Récamier* (Louvre) being famous.

Degas, Edgar (1834–1917). French painter, pastelist and sculptor. A splendid draughtsman, he produced masterly interpretations of the poses and movement of ballet dancers in oil paintings and pastels, as well as brilliant and unconventional studies of the nude.

Delacroix, Ferdinand Victor Eugène (1789–1867). French painter who represents the Romantic spirit in French art. He excelled in exotic and historical subjects (*The Death of Sardanapalus, Women of Algiers*) and his *Liberty at the Barricades* celebrates the revolution of 1830.

Dobson, William (1610–1646). Portrait painter, born in London and employed by Van Dyck but noted as one of the first painters of truly English character. His best known work is his *Endymion Porter* (National Gallery).

Duccio (di Buoninsegna, 13th century). Painter of the Sienese school, one of those who broke away from Byzantine conventions, and a precursor of Giotto.

Dürer, Albrecht (1471–1528). German painter and engraver, born at Nuremberg, the greatest

Renaissance master outside Italy. His engravings on copper (*Melencolia, Knight, Death and the Devil*) and on wood (the *Apocalypse* series), his minute studies of nature, his water-colour landscapes as well as his portraits are all works of original genius.

Ensor, James (1860–1949). Anglo-Flemish painter and engraver, noted for imaginative works introducing macabre figures of carnival. He has some affinity with the surrealists.

Eyck, Hubert and **Jan van** (15th century). Painter brothers of the Flemish school who traditionally collaborated on the master-work *The Adoration of the Lamb* (Ghent). Little is known of Hubert, but Jan emerges clearly as a great artist in religious pictures and portraiture, and a brilliant pioneer of the oil technique.

Fantin-Latour, Henri (1836–1904). French painter and lithographer, chiefly noted for his accomplished flower and still life paintings.

Fragonard, Jean Honoré (1732–1806). French painter who, like Boucher, expressed the artificial charm of the Louis XV period (e.g. in *The Swing*, Wallace Collection, London). A prolific and versatile genius, he excelled in landscape and scenes of everyday life as well as gallant subjects.

Frith, William Powell (1819–1909). English painter who turned from historical subjects to portrayal of the Victorian social scene. His fame rests mainly on his ever-popular *Derby Day*, 1858 (National Gallery) his *Ramsgate Sands* and *Railway Station* being in similar vein.

Fuseli, Henry (1741–1828). Swiss-born painter who settled in England and is noted for his imaginative paintings of Shakespearean subjects and drawings in a fantastic vein.

Gainsborough, Thomas (1727–1788). English painter, born at Sudbury. His greatness equally appears in portraits and landscapes. Early landscapes represent his native Suffolk (e.g. *Cornard Wood*), later landscapes are imaginary compositions, e.g. *The Watering Place*. In portraiture his *Blue Boy*, *Duchess of Devonshire* and *The Morning Walk* are among many masterpieces.

Gauguin, Paul (1848–1903). French painter, a post-Impressionist, whose work is marked by brilliant colour and a definite pattern of design. He produced notable paintings in Brittany, but is best known by his paintings of natives in the South Seas where he died.

Géricault, Théodore (1791–1824). French painter, leader with Delacroix of Romanticism. He is noted for his spirited pictures of horses (including a race at Epsom). His masterpiece was the *Raft of the Medusa* (Louvre) which dramatically depicts the survivors of shipwreck.

Ghirlandaio (Domenico Bigordi, 1449–1494). Florentine painter, master of Michelangelo and one of the leading Renaissance masters. His greatest works are religious frescoes at Florence, e.g. scenes from the life of St. John the Baptist and of the Virgin in the church of S. Maria Novella, but he also painted remarkable portraits.

Giorgione (Giorgio Barbarelli, 1477–1510). Venetian painter who first gave that sensuous richness to oil paint which inspired his longer-lived contemporary Titian. Masterpieces among the world's greatest pictures are *The Storm* (Accademia, Venice) and the *Concert Champêtre* (Louvre).

Giotto (Ambrogio di Bondone, c. 1266–1337). One of the greatest Italian masters, painter, architect and sculptor. He gave to fresco painting a grandeur of style combined with dramatic expression which long guided the course of Italian art. Frescoes illustrating the life of St. Francis (Assisi) and the New Testament story (Arena Chapel, Padua) are famous works.

Girtin, Thomas (1773–1802). Water-colour painter, born in London. He brought a breadth of vision into landscape painting which influenced both Turner and Constable. *The White House, Chelsea* (Tate Gallery) and *Durham* (Whitworth Gallery, Manchester) are beautiful examples of his art.

Gogh, Vincent van (1853–1890). Dutch painter who gave an extraordinary and personal intensity to oil colour and brushwork, in landscape, portraits and still life. In a short period in France he produced memorable views of Arles, his famous *Sunflowers*, such vivid portraits as his *Zouave*, and *L'Arlésienne*. His letters and the drawings with them show how each picture was conceived.

Goes, Hugo van der (c. 1440–1482). One of the great Flemish masters of the 15th century whose religious paintings show original composition and a keen sense of human character. Famous works are the *Portinari Altarpiece* (Uffizi, Florence) and the *Death of the Virgin* (Bruges).

Gonçalves, Nuño (15th century). A great solitary Portuguese master. He painted religious figure compositions on a large scale in oil, which may be compared with those of van Eyck.

Goya, Francisco de (1746–1828). Great Spanish painter and graphic artist. His work is noted for its brilliant and often satiric observation. He painted scenes of Spanish life—bullfights, ceremonies, festivals and remarkable portraits, unsparing in truth; while his etched plates, the *Caprices* and *Miseries of War* were inspired by the Napoleonic invasion and by his critical view of society. The Prado, Madrid contains much of his best work.

Greco, El (Domenicos Theotocopuli, 1541–1614). Cretan by birth and trained at Venice by the study of Titian and Tintoretto, this painter, known as "the Greek", settled at Toledo and ranks as one of the greatest Spanish masters. Spiritual fervour and dignified portraiture mark his masterpiece *The Burial of Count Orgaz* (Toledo). *The Agony in the Garden* (National Gallery) is impressive and typical.

Grünewald, Matthias (otherwise M. Neithardt, c. 1455–1528). Great German painter, contemporary with Dürer, but more expressive of the medieval German spirit in art. His few remaining works include notably the *Isenheim Altarpiece* (Colmar) and *Christ Mocked* (Munich).

Hals, Frans (c. 1580–1666). Painter of the Dutch school, working at Haarlem, and noted for brilliant portraits of which the *Laughing Cavalier* (Wallace Collection, London) is a famous example. He painted the prosperous middle-class (*The Officers' Banquet, Haarlem*), bohemian types (*Hille Bobbe*, Berlin) and a more austere masterpiece of his later years is the *Regents of the St. Elizabeth Hospital*.

Hiroshige (1797–1858). Japanese graphic artist, noted for his colour prints of landscape in Japan. Their calculated simplicity of colour and design had considerable influence on 19th-century European art.

Hobbema, Meindert (1638–1709). Dutch landscape painter, a follower of Ruysdael. His best work is *The Avenue, Middelharnis* (National Gallery).

Hogarth, William (1697–1764). One of the great English artists, painter and engraver, born in London. From small portrait groups—"conversation pieces"—he turned to those scenes of social life painted and engraved in series, of which the best is *Marriage à la Mode* (1745) in the Tate Gallery. *Calais Gate* and the *Shrimp Girl* (National Gallery) are among his masterpieces. His written *Analysis of Beauty* is still of interest.

Hokusai (1760–1849). Japanese graphic artist, noted for his colour prints of Japanese life and landscape, and also for brush drawings of figures, birds and animals, full of vitality, which have given him international fame.

Holbein, Hans (the Younger)(1497–1543). German painter who settled in London and became court painter to Henry VIII. Great works are his *Portrait of Erasmus* (Louvre) and *Christina, Duchess of Milan* (National Gallery) and the drawings of men and women of the Tudor court (Royal Collection, Windsor).

Hooch, Pieter de (1629–1681). Dutch painter, working at Delft, famous for his views of Dutch interiors and courtyards.

Hunt, William Holman (1827–1910). Painter, born in London, a Pre-Raphaelite who adhered strictly to the watchword "Truth to Nature". This is well exemplified by his *The Hireling Shepherd* and *Scapegoat*.

Ingres, Jean Auguste Dominique (1780–1867). French painter and draughtsman and a follower of David in upholding classic principles. Famous pictures are the *Apotheosis of Homer*, *La Source* and *L'Odalisque* in the Louvre. His portrait pencil drawings are of matchless beauty.

John, Augustus (1878–). British painter, noted for his portraits, of which his *Madame Suggia* (Tate Gallery) is a fine example, romantic figure studies with Irish or Welsh background, and masterly drawings and etchings.

Keene, Charles Samuel (1823–1891). English graphic artist, widely known for his drawings in *Punch*, but even more esteemed for beautiful pen studies of figures and landscape.

Klee, Paul (1879–1940). German-Swiss artist who exploited combinations of line and colour fancifully suggesting plants, animals or dream-like scenes.

La Tour, Georges de (1593–1652). French painter of religious subjects in which impressive use is made of torch-light effects. He is now considered one of the great 17th-century painters.

La Tour, Maurice Quentin de (1704–1788). French artist noted for his pastel portraits of 18th-century French royalty and society. He bequeathed a large number of works to his native town, St. Quentin.

Le Nain. Name of three brothers, **Antoine** (c. 1585–1648), **Louis** (1593–1645) and **Mathieu** (1607–1677), who often collaborated in paintings of French peasant life which show both human understanding and delicacy of execution.

Leonardo da Vinci (1452–1519). Florentine artist, one of the greatest figures of the Italian Renaissance. Many of his projects were unrealized but his few paintings include unique masterpieces: the *Last Supper* (1498) on the refectory wall of the Convent of S. Maria delle Grazie, Milan, much deteriorated through his use of an experimental oil medium; the *Mona Lisa* (Louvre) and two versions of the *Madonna of the Rocks* (Louvre and National Gallery). The larger part of his remaining work consists of exquisite drawings, often connected with his scientific studies and inventions. A magnificent large drawing is the cartoon for a *Madonna and*

Child with St. Anne (Royal Academy, London). His *Note Books* may be studied as a revelation of his thought.

Lewis, Wyndham (1884–1957). English painter and writer, leader of the pre-1914 movement called Vorticism, related to the continental Cubism and Futurism. His portrait of T. S. Eliot and his imaginative composition *Barcelona* (Tate Gallery) are notable among his pictorial works.

Lippi, Fra Filippo (1406–1469). Florentine painter of religious subjects noted for serene and harmonious compositions, e.g. the *Annunciation* (National Gallery). His son, **Filippino Lippi** (1457–1504), worked with Botticelli.

Manet, Edouard (1832–1883). Born in Paris, noted for works in which old master themes were treated with modern realism, e.g. his *Olympia* and *Déjeuner sur l'Herbe* (Louvre). He was also influenced by his younger contemporaries the Impressionists. A late masterpiece is his *Bar aux Folies-Bergère* (Courtauld Collection).

Mantegna, Andrea (1431–1506). Italian painter and engraver associated with the Venetian school. His work has a severe dignity derived from the study of ancient Roman sculpture. Among his masterpieces is the *Triumph of Julius Caesar* (Hampton Court).

Masaccio (Tommaso Guidi, 1401–1428). Florentine painter working in the spirit of Giotto but adding fresh qualities in perspective and the sculpture-like modelling of solid form, as in his frescoes for the Church of the Carmine, Florence.

Matisse, Henri (1869–1954). French painter, noted for his use of pure colour, a leader of the movement known as Fauvism. A notable work is his *La Danse* (Barnes Foundation).

Memlinc, Hans (c. 1435–1494). One of the great early Flemish painters who excelled both in religious paintings, delightful in detail and landscape background, and also in portraits.

Messina, Antonello da (15th century). Italian painter, born at Messina, celebrated as having introduced into Italy the mode of oil painting practised by van Eyck. A self-portrait in red cap is in the National Gallery.

Michelangelo (Buonarroti, 1475–1564). Great Florentine artist, painter, sculptor and architect. Though primarily a sculptor, he was urged by Pope Julius II to decorate the ceiling of the Sistine Chapel with paintings. These (1508–1512) and the later wall fresco, the *Last Judgement* (1537–1541), form perhaps the most stupendous achievement in the history of pictorial art. Michelangelo was interested only in the human figure, and alike in sculpture paintings and drawings shows a complete mastery of form, gesture and movement.

Millais, Sir John Everett (1829–1896). English Pre-Raphaelite painter, mainly esteemed for his minutely detailed early work, as in his *Christ in the House of his Parents* (Tate Gallery) and *Ophelia* (National Gallery).

Monet, Claude (1840–1926). French landscape painter, leader of the Impressionists, devoted to the rendering of light and shade by colour and to the direct study of nature. His *Nymphéas* (Tate Gallery) is a typical study of open-air effect.

Morland, George (1763–1804). English painter of rustic scenes, showing village inns, cottages, farm buildings and animals, executed with great facility.

Munch, Edvard (1863–1943). Norwegian painter and graphic artist, whose somewhat sombre style had much influence in Europe and encouraged Expressionism.

Nash, Paul (1889–1946). English painter of landscape and still life, noted also for striking paintings of the 1914–1918 war and again of the last war. Surrealism encouraged the imaginative style of his later work.

Nicholson. English painters, father and son, both **Sir William Nicholson** (1872-1949) and **Ben Nicholson** (1894–) being especially notable for still life, though the latter works in a semi-abstract and geometric style.

Pacher, Michael (c. 1430–1498). German painter and wood sculptor, noted for boldly composed altarpieces, Gothic in spirit but introducing striking effects of space and perspective.

Picasso, Pablo (1881–). Spanish artist and leader of the "School of Paris", brilliantly versatile and prolific. His influence has been world-wide. With Georges Braque an originator of Cubism, he has not, however, been confined to one style or form of art. Paintings, etchings, book illustration, design for ballets and for ceramics, and sculpture are aspects of his activity. His early pictures of acrobats and circus performers, his Cubist still lifes, his bitter *Guernica* (Modern Museum of Art, New York), his returns to naturalistic portraiture and drawing, show his remarkable variety.

Piero della Francesca (c. 1416–1492). Great Italian artist of the early Renaissance, the author of compositions which uniquely combine an abstract system of geometric proportion with human feeling. His masterpieces of fresco painting are in the church of St. Francis, Arezzo. An early work, the *Baptism of Christ* and a superb *Nativity* are in the National Gallery.

Pisanello (Antonio Pisano, fl. early 15th century). Italian painter and maker of portrait medallions. He combines a Gothic feeling for detail with the interest in nature of the Renaissance. A small masterpiece in this vein is his *Vision of St. Eustace* (National Gallery). He made magnificent drawings of animals.

Pollaiuolo. Name of two artist brothers, **Antonio** and **Piero**, distinguished in the history of Florentine art. They worked together, but **Antonio Pollaiuolo** (1426–1498) is accounted the more original of the two. Though also goldsmith, engraver and sculptor he is mainly known by paintings showing a study of anatomy and physical movement typical of the Renaissance. *The Martyrdom of St. Sebastian* (National Gallery) is an example.

Poussin, Nicolas (1594–1665). French painter, mainly working in Rome and there influenced both by antique sculpture and the Renaissance masters in perfecting a "classical" style. His *Arcadian Shepherds* (Louvre) well conveys this aim, but examples of his power in figure composition are widely distributed and are to be seen in the Wallace and Dulwich Gallery collections, London, among others.

Raphael (Raffaello Santi, 1483–1520). Great Italian painter, born at Urbino. He is noted for a series of Madonnas in the graceful style of his master, Perugino, but his genius attained its full fruition in Rome, where he was inspired by Michelangelo and Leonardo. His greatest works are frescoes for a series of rooms in the Vatican including the wonderful *School of Athens* and *Parnassus*. His Cartoons (Victoria and Albert Museum) for tapestries in the Sistine Chapel are to painting what the Parthenon frieze is to sculpture. A famous portrait is his *Baldassare Castiglione* (Louvre).

Rembrandt van Rijn (1606–1669). Greatest of Dutch artists, whose genius is displayed in portraits, religious compositions, landscape and a vast number of etchings and drawings showing the wide range of his powers and interests. His masterpieces include the so-called *Night Watch* (Rijksmuseum, Amsterdam), the *Anatomy Lesson* (Rijksmuseum), the *Entombment* (Munich) and many self-portraits. His house in Amsterdam is a Rembrandt museum.

Reni, Guido (1575–1642). Italian painter and etcher, a follower of L. Carracci, noted for graceful but mannered compositions, the most famous being his *Aurora and the Hours* for the Respigliosi Palace, Rome.

Renoir, Auguste (1841–1919). French painter of figure and landscape. One of the Impressionist group, he painted many works full of sunlight and the feeling of open air, though diverging in later years from Impressionist aims. Famous works are *La Loge* (National Gallery), *Le Moulin de la Galette* (Louvre) and *The Judgement of Paris*.

Reynolds, Sir Joshua (1723–1792). Portrait painter whose work combines the fruit of studying the great European masters with an original and natural capacity. *Nelly O'Brien* (Wallace Collection) and his *Dr Johnson* (Tate Gallery) well illustrate his powers. His written *Discourses* are an admirable statement of the enlightened 18th-century view of art.

Romney, George (1734–1802). A rival of Reynolds among 18th-century portrait painters whose ideal type was Emma Hart (Lady Hamilton) of whom he painted many studies.

Rossetti, Dante Gabriel (1828–1882). Pre-Raphaelite painter and poet born in London. His early *Annunciation* (National Gallery) reflects one aspect of Pre-Raphaelite aims. Much of his best work is in water colours, medieval in feeling.

Rouault, Georges (1871–1945). French painter, whose work has something of the quality of stained glass, an appropriate medium for expressing this artist's sense of religion.

Roublev, Andrew (c. 1360–1430). Russian monk who painted icons in the Byzantine style and is noted for a beautiful *Holy Trinity* in the S. Serge Convent, near Moscow.

Rousseau, Henri ("Le Douanier", 1844–1910). French amateur painter who became noted late in life for works with a naïve quality of vision, shown especially in dreamlike compositions of imagined tropical forests.

Rousseau, Théodore (1812–1867). French landscape painter, a principal member of the Barbizon School who painted poetic woodland scenes in the region of Fontainebleau.

Rowlandson, Thomas (1756–1827). Graphic artist, born in London, whose water-colours represent the varied humours of late 18th-century English life with great verve and an admirable feeling for composition. His *Vauxhall Gardens* is a famous work.

Rubens, Peter Paul (1577–1640). Great Flemish painter, excelling in portraiture, landscape, and religious, historical and mythological compositions on a large scale. Among his masterpieces are *The Descent from the Cross* (Antwerp), *The Rape of the Daughters of Leucippus* (Munich), *The Flemish Kermesse* (Louvre) and *Peace and War*, *Chapeau de Paille*, and *Château de Steen* (National Gallery).

Ruysdael, Jacob van (1629–1682). Dutch landscape painter, famous for woodland scenes, poetic and sombre, which greatly inspired the English landscape painters Gainsborough, Crome and Constable and in France the Barbizon school.

Seurat, Georges (1859–1891). Following the Impressionists, Seurat was one of those who brought back firm and considered design into painting, though using a method of dividing colour into the primaries, red, yellow and blue which was a logical conclusion of the Impressionist technique. *La Baignade* (Tate Gallery) combines monumental conception with sunny atmosphere.

Sickert, Walter Richard (1860–1942). English painter, influenced by Whistler and Degas, who developed a personal Impressionist style. He is noted for pictures of Dieppe and Venice, of London music halls and interiors, and had an inspiring effect on a younger generation.

Signorelli, Luca (c. 1441–1523). Italian painter, pupil of Piero della Francesca, and admired by Michelangelo, who made a special feature of expressive and characteristic gesture. Frescoes in the Cathedral, Orvieto are his main work (*Pan* was a masterpiece destroyed in Berlin in the second World War).

Steer, Philip Wilson (1860–1944). English painter noted for landscapes in oil and water colour. *Yachts*, *Walberswick* and *Chepstow Castle* (Tate Gallery) are among his main works.

Stevens, Alfred (1817–1875). Sculptor, designer and draughtsman. The Tate Gallery contains a large number of studies for his Wellington monument and other works.

Stubbs, George (1724–1806). English painter of horses and rural scenes. He engraved the plates for a work on *The Anatomy of the Horse*. *The Reapers* (collection of Lord Bearsted) is one of his outstanding works.

Tiepolo, Giovanni Battista (1696–1770). Last of the great Venetian fresco painters, he is noted for daringly theatrical effects of perspective and grouping in large-scale compositions such as the scenes from the life of Cleopatra (Labia Palace, Venice).

Tintoretto (Jacopo Robusti, 1518–1594). Great Venetian painter, who developed with prodigious force the idea of movement in space. Religious themes on a large scale, dynamic in energy, e.g. his *Last Supper* (Venice, Scuola di San Rocco) and imaginative compositions, *St. George and the Dragon*, *The Origin of the Milky Way* (National Gallery) provided his great masterpieces.

Titian (Tiziano Vecelli, c. 1487–1576). Great Venetian painter and a main inspiration of European painting. He explored the full range of the oil medium in religious and imaginative works and in portraiture. Among his masterpieces are *Sacred and Profane Love* (Rome, Borghese Gallery), *The Assumption* (Venice, Church of the Frari), *Bacchus and Ariadne* (National Gallery), *Portrait of Charles V* (Munich).

Toulouse-Lautrec, Comte Henri de (1864–1901). Painter and graphic designer, famous for scenes of sophisticated life and the Parisian *demi-monde*.

Influenced by Japanese prints he produced brilliant lithographed posters for the Moulin Rouge and other resorts, masterpieces of their kind.

Turner, Joseph Mallord William (1775–1851). English painter, perhaps the greatest of landscape painters, in both oil and water-colour. Beginning with topographical subjects he next sought to vie with old masters—the marine painting of the Dutch and especially Claude's rendering of light—and his later works were a superb personal expression in colour. Masterpieces include his *Calais Pier*, *Frosty Morning*, *The Sun of Venice* and *Rain, Steam and Speed* (National Gallery).

Uccello (Paolo Dono, c. 1396–c. 1479). Florentine painter, one of the early students of perspective. He is noted for a series of battle scenes, of which one is the famous *Rout of San Romano* (National Gallery).

Van Dyck, Sir Anthony (1599–1641). Flemish-born painter, favourite pupil of Rubens, who became court painter to Charles I and is famous for his portraits of the king and his queen, Henrietta Maria. He made a number of fine etched portraits.

Velazquez, Diego (1599–1660). Great Spanish painter, a master of realism, court painter to Philip IV. His masterpieces include *Los Borrachos* (The Drinkers), *The Surrender of Breda*, *The Maids of Honour* and *The Tapestry Weavers* (Prado, Madrid) and also many magnificent portraits of the king, queen and royal children as well as characters of the court, buffoons and dwarfs.

Vermeer, Jan (1632–1675). Regarded as next to Rembrandt the greatest Dutch painter. Masterpieces include *The Artist in his Studio* (Vienna), *The Little Street* (Rijksmuseum, Amsterdam), *View of Delft* (Mauritshuis, Hague) and *Lady standing at the Virginals* (National Gallery), all showing a beautiful lucidity of design and colour.

Veronese (Paolo Caliari, 1528–1588). Decorative painter of the Venetian school, famous for sumptuous works on a large scale. *The Marriage at Cana* (Louvre) assembling a vast number of figures in contemporary dress against an architectural background is one of his most noted works.

Watteau, Antoine (1684–1721). Great French painter, famous for his pictures of characters of Italian comedy (e.g. his *Pierrot*, Louvre) and of courtly open-air entertainments (*fêtes galantes*), like *The Embarkation for Cythera* (Louvre). His figure drawings in black and red chalk are equally works of great beauty.

Weyden, Rogier van der (c. 1399–1464). Early Flemish master, famous for the natural expression and grouping in his altarpieces. A notable work is *The Descent from the Cross* (Madrid).

Whistler, James McNeill (1834–1903). American-born painter, pastellist and etcher, famous for works in which form and colour are selected and simplified with exquisite care. His famous works include portraits—*Thomas Carlyle* (Glasgow), *The Artist's Mother* (Louvre), and Nocturnes of which *Old Battersea Bridge* (Tate Gallery) is the most celebrated.

Witz, Conrad (15th century). German painter who worked at Basle and is especially noted for his *Miraculous draught of Fish* (Geneva) which introduces an elaborate and existing landscape background.

Zeuxis (5th century B.C.). Famous Greek painter of antiquity. No works by him are known but a fanciful story of birds pecking his painted grapes suggest that realistic still life was among them.

Zoffany, Johann (1733–1810). German-born painter who settled in England and is well known for admirable conversation pieces.

Zurbaran, Francisco (1598–c. 1664). Spanish painter noted for sombre religious pictures of great force, as well as for portraits and still life. *A Franciscan* (National Gallery) is typical.

INDEX

157

158

PRINTED FOR THE PUBLISHERS BY
JARROLD AND SONS LTD NORWICH

EUROPEAN PAINTING & P[			
Date:	ITALIAN	FRENCH	FLEMISH
1600	CARAVAGGIO DOMENICHINO GUIDO RENI GUERCINO	P. DE CHAMPAIGNE } G. DE LA TOUR	RUBENS VAN DYCK
25			
50			SNYDERS JORDAENS
	SALVATOR ROSA	POUSSIN	TENIERS
75		CLAUDE LE BRUN	
1700	MAGNASCO	WATTEAU	
25		BOUCHER	
		CHARDIN	
50	TIEPOLO CANALETTO	FRAGONARD	
75	GUARDI LONGHI	H. ROBERT J. L. DAVID	
1800		GERICAULT	
25		DELACROIX INGRES COROT MILLET	
50		COURBET MANET MONET	
75		RENOIR DEGAS LAUTREC CEZANNE	
1900	"Futurism"	GAUGUIN	
25	MODIGLIANI CHIRICO	MATISSE BRAQUE School of Paris	ENSOR